D0735532

The Mount of Olives

11 Declarations to an Extraordinary Life

MICHAEL V. IVANOV

Copyright © 2017 Michael V. Ivanov

All rights reserved.

This book or any portion thereof

may not be reproduced or used in any manner whatsoever

without the express written permission of the publisher

except for the use of brief quotations in a book review.

ISBN: 0-692-91365-3
ISBN-13: 978-0-692-91365-9

www.SPEAKLIFE365.com

Special discounts are available on quantity purchases by corporations, associations, and others. For details, contact the publisher at the web address above.

Dedication

To my precious family and my precious woman…

I fear that if I attempt to put my love for you into words, I will fall short of what my heart truly feels for you.

Not a day goes by that I don't thank God for every one of you.

To my precious reader…

Nothing gets me more excited than when someone sets out on their own path to seek a better way to live.

We all want different things but, in the end, all the same things matter to us.

Never quit searching, never settle, and never stop seeking your greatest purpose. It is in the struggle of your search that your purpose will be revealed and you will find the extraordinary life.

As you read, take these declarations and speak them over your own life.

Be extraordinary!

-Michael

Contents

Chapter 1. The boy on the hill

"Imbecile!!"

The boy was startled out of a deep sleep and quickly jumped to his feet.

"Imbecile!!"

The soldier shouted again, this time stepping up just inches from the boy. The smell of strong drink came from his breath as his beady eyes scanned up and down the boy's form. Scrunched brows kept his helmet from falling over his face and the side flaps bounced on either side of his sweaty scowl. He panted from the climb up the hill.

"Worthless mute! Even this simple task you cannot handle! And you wanted to join the army?" Before the man even finished the sentence a hard slap struck the boy's face and he staggered to the ground from the unexpected blow.

The dusty leather sandal slammed against his throat as the man pinned him to the dirt. "If I catch you sleeping on your post again," he sneered, "not only will you not get your pay but I'll have you hung up there beside him!" The foot then landed hard against the boy's ribs.

The soldier marched off, swearing aloud, and the boy lifted himself off of the ground. A metallic taste filled his mouth and he pressed his tongue against the inside of his cheek to stop the bleeding.

Brushing himself off with shaky hands, he picked up the belt with the sheathed sword, and buckled it around his waist. He grabbed his old pouch, the animal skin darkened by years in the sun, and slung it over his shoulder.

He was disgusted with himself for falling asleep and then his anger turned to the soldier.

How can a man like _that_ be in the army but I can't join!?

He sat down at the foot of the wood beam, still holding his cheek, and stared out into the hills as the sun neared the horizon. Down in the city, most of the torches left burning overnight had already died. A new day was beginning. It was a cold morning and the boy watched his breath swirl before him and vanish with each exhale. He hadn't planned on staying all night and shivered without an extra layer to cover his tunic.

The night before had marked his third shift on the hill and usually by this time, the criminals were already dead. He turned and looked up at the man hanging above him, chest still moving.

This one wants to live, he thought and turned back to the hills, again falling deep in thought as the sun finally peeked over the horizon.

***

Three months ago the boy turned 17, the age he would be considered a man. At 17, he could join the military and fight. He had admired the Roman soldiers since he was a child. It was everything that made a man, a man. The silver helmets topped by the crimson crest and the chest plates gleaming in the sun as they marched in and out of the city were more than enough reason to enlist. He would stop and marvel as the soldiers marched by, steps perfectly in sync.

Raised in an orphanage where he didn't know who his mother or father were, he had plenty of other reasons to join. After all, he had been a burden to people all of his life. A burden to the citizens of Rome whose taxes paid for his food and shelter at the orphanage. A burden to the women who raised him and prepared his meals, and obviously, a burden to his mother who had left him on the steps of the temple as an infant.

His plan was foolproof. As soon as he joined, he would go from burden to glory. He would be a soldier and earn a soldier's wages. With these he would save enough money to buy a plot of land in the hills outside of the city. He would grow his olive trees and sell the oil and olives.

He would be a wealthy man and give the orphanage his time and gold so that others would not grow up in the loneliness he himself was imprisoned to.

And then there was Licinia, the only girl at the orphanage. Her unusual green eyes sparkled. Her kindness made her prettier still. Since the day she slapped the bully who mocked the boy for not being able to speak, she'd been his friend.

One day she would help him till the fields and care for the trees. All he needed to do was convince her of this dream and he would surely win her over. Once he joined the army, everything would fall into place.

The day came and he entered the office of the general. His excitement soon turned to a trembling terror and his palms grew sweaty as each question from the general only led to more mocking. His big brown eyes studied the general's face hoping to be understood, but found only sarcasm. When all he could do was nod or shake his head to each question, the room, quickly filling with curious centurions, erupted into laughter.

The boy was born a mute.

The general hadn't bothered reading the pleading words the boy had scribbled on a torn piece of a scroll.

He would never be able to fight alongside others. A

Roman soldier must be able to echo orders given in the heat of battle and a mute boy would create a weak spot. His head spun as the general explained.

"We do need an execution guard, however," the general finally offered. "The pay is not much but for a useless boy like yourself whom the gods haven't favored, you can't ask for more."

***

Here he was. On the hill just north of the city gate, waiting for the man charged with murder to die. His job was to watch over the guilty and ensure their accomplices didn't sneak up in the night and take down those being executed.

A common Roman execution, resulting in humiliating, excruciating pain, and a slow death. Some died from the pain within hours. Stripped naked and nailed to the cross with their arms stretched out, their feet were nailed together and pinned below them at an angle. Others lasted a few days, until they could no longer shift their back up against the wood for another breath. Their arms were stretched wide, causing them much difficulty and pain to hold themselves up. Eventually unable to breathe, they would suffocate.

The other guards were not patient: "We get paid for each body, not for our time spent up here. If you break their knees, they are gone within a few hours," they said. "Besides, it puts them out of their misery."

They do not have the courage required to become real soldiers but they can kill a helpless man without a second thought, the boy thought with disgust.

He looked up at the man whose eyes had already been closed for hours. Only a slight rising and deflating of the chest revealed any sign of life. He shuddered at the thought of clubbing the man's knees; he would never be able to live with himself. It didn't matter how long he had to stay up here, he would wait for death.

***

In his months as a guard on the hill, he watched one life after another leave with a final breath and he often thought about these men. Most of the convicted were poor: slaves, bandits, thieves, and murderers who had been dealt a bad hand in life by the gods and chose to take a path that, ultimately, led them here.

Others were wealthy, prominent men of high political status who were convicted of treason, bribery, or conspiracy.

Up on the cross, naked with his hands pierced through the bone, it didn't matter how much gold or fame a man had collected in his lifetime. The boy could not distinguish between one and the next without the plank that listed each man's criminal convictions.

Some of them begged for help. Every time this happened he distanced himself until he could see them but no longer hear their screams for mercy. He learned quickly to avoid making eye contact and tried hard to detach himself from the thought of them being human.

At times it was more than he could handle. His knees would grow weak, his body would begin to shake and he'd vomit on the ground as the fear paralyzed him. But with time, it became easier and he learned to control himself, especially when the soldiers came around to check on him.

It was almost midday when he walked up to the foot of the cross again. He pushed the body with the back end of his spear and saw that it was limp. The entire weight of the man was now sagging on the nails.

Thus began the easy part of his job, for he no longer feared a conversation with the criminal. He pulled the nails for their next use and the body dropped to the ground. Wrapping the man with a sheet, he rolled him onto his stretcher and pulled the stretcher behind him down towards the city. He delivered the body for burial and collected his pay.

He stopped at a lone tent in the market on his way back to the orphanage. The rest of the merchants had folded up for the day. Pointing to the cheapest wine skin, he pulled a few coins from his pouch.

At the orphanage he climbed to the roof where the women often sun-dried their carpets and clothes. It was his favorite spot and he spent a lot of time up here when he needed to get away from the others. From here he could see the hills above the city, which formed a peaceful background in the distance as if to mock the insignificant worries of the people below. Licinia had joined him here many times and he loved to listen to her voice and marvel at her beauty as she shared her dreams.

She would talk and he would listen, glancing away quickly when she caught him staring.

He was jealous of the other boys. They could speak. They spoke freely about everything that came to mind, even things that made them look foolish, which he found odd. They compared muscle size and apparently knew exactly what women found attractive in a man.

Perhaps when you are able to speak, you can't think at the same time.

Just like all of them, he had so much to say. He wished he could speak about his dreams and the things he thought about, but he could only listen.

There were times in the orphanage classroom when his frustrations would erupt and he would scream, silently, tears rolling down his face as others read aloud. He couldn't form words like they did. And he couldn't understand why.

That early pain gave him a desire to communicate any way possible and he began to read and write much sooner than the rest of the orphans. But it was far worse now not to be able to speak to Licinia than it had ever been at school. She was the only one he really ever wanted to speak to anyway.

***

It was only a few more months until he would have to leave the orphanage and go out on his own. He was considered a man now and the woman who had raised him here had told him he could stay only until he was able to find a place to live. All his glorious former plans had been based around joining the Roman army.

Now I am destined to join the rest of the beggars wandering the streets. Slaves have it better than I do, he thought.

The sun was starting to set and just as the day was fading, his dream of olive fields and riches began to fade with it.

He took another swig from the half-empty wine skin. Propped up with his back against the clay wall, heated by a day full of sun, he closed his eyes and let the last bit of warmth kiss him on the cheeks.

The sun, all of nature, the hills outside of the city where he spent much of his time, had treated him better than any gods of Rome that he learned about as a child. Tears came down his face as a familiar anger swept over him.

He threw the wine skin and watched it skid across the dusty clay roof. Every curse word he had ever learned came through his mind bringing more anger and tears with it.

"Lucky, Successful."

This was the meaning of his name in Latin.

I am about as lucky and successful as bull shit stuck to the bottom of the emperor's shoe!

I can't sell in the market place. I haven't been raised with any skills like the men in the blacksmith shops or the stables. I can't earn enough gold to buy land for my olive trees… I might as well become a beggar. Licinia won't want anything to do with a useless mute anyway.

He thought again of the general and the centurions who laughed at him and it only kindled his frustration and feeling of rejection. There was nothing left for him here. All hope of success had faded and he had awakened to a new reality—drowning in a bottomless sea without a soul in sight to toss a rope.

His dream had fueled him for so long it felt strange to lose direction and any sense of purpose.

He needed to leave. He needed to get as far away as possible from his failures, the pity of others, the identity that was his life here in Rome.

The sun set and darkness began to creep in. The boy picked himself up from his perch and stumbled down the steps to his cot.

Chapter 2.

A journey begins

It was still dark outside when the boy rose and rolled his bedding tightly, placing his sword carefully in the middle and securing it with a string. Romans were not popular in territories they had conquered and he did not want to be mistaken for a soldier wherever he ended up. He wanted to return the sword assigned to him for protection on the hill but he feared being laughed at again, this time for quitting. Besides, having it on his back gave him a sense of safety.

He crept out the main entrance to the orphanage, stepped into the courtyard, and headed for the front gate. He had only taken a few steps when he heard a familiar voice from behind.

"Felix!" Licinia whispered as she stood in the doorway. He turned around to look at her for a moment and then stared at the ground. He had wanted to tell her goodbye the evening before but did not want to let her know he was not coming back.

As she stepped into the moonlight, he saw tears lining her face. He remembered when they were both 11, and she taught him about olive trees. "Sometimes they take 5 to 8 years to produce fruit," she had said. And he fell in love with these trees, barren and useless for so long just like he had been. But when they became ripe, they produced an abundance of fruit. He would one day do the same with his life.

That day they both ran to the market where he stole a few olive seeds and planted them in the hills outside the city.

She had seen his frustration when the other boys got jobs in the market, temples and government palaces, and he was turned away each time. She had seen him try again and again to do what all the normal boys did, only to fail harder each time and endure yet more rejection.

Here in Rome, anybody with a disability was considered a hindrance to society and he was certainly treated as such.

The girl leaned in and kissed him on the cheek. *"Just when it seems like the olive tree will never produce, it brings forth more fruit than can be contained,"* she whispered. She turned around and stepped into the darkness of the home.

The boy stood and stared at the entrance for a moment, then turned and headed down the quiet street. His mind screamed to turn back as the familiar walk suddenly felt lonelier. But his feet kept moving forward.

Flickering torches, still lit at the door posts, were the

only sign of life in the soundless streets. As he reached the gate he so often passed through, he brushed his hand against the cold clay walls for the last time and headed west towards Fiumicino.

He had only been to Fiumicino once as a younger boy, traveling there with a few of the women who ran the orphanage. They needed his help to load up and haul back a supply cart from the ships. He had strong arms and enjoyed the challenge of the labor.

He recalled it would take nearly five hours to get there by foot.

The sky behind was brightening as he walked down the road. Just as the road began to curve he turned for a final glance at the city. He'd spent his entire life there and it was all he knew. In the hours before dawn, the city looked cold and uninviting. And he knew he would not be missed. Only the girl in the orphanage would even remember him. He touched his cheek where she'd kissed him and turned toward his destination again.

The road carved through the dips in the hills and to the east, the mountain range loomed in the sky. Jagged cliffs still wrapped in dusk made him feel small as he passed by.

***

Salty air filled his nostrils as he approached the city. A cool breeze coming from the Tyrrhenian Sea blew against his face, filling him with a new energy. He made his way towards the boat docks. He knew he did not have enough coins to pay for a trip but perhaps he could work on a boat as payment.

I'll go anywhere a ship can go, as long as it sails away from Rome.

As he sat at the docks and watched the slaves loading bags onto a ship, he realized the flaw in his plan. How could he convince someone to let him on board in exchange for work when they had all the help they needed for no payment?

A man approached, and sat next to him on a post. He was dressed in unusual clothes, which the boy had seen before. The long robe hardly seemed comfortable in the heat of the day but it certainly was elegant with the bright colors weaved around the seams of the silky material. The man looked like the people who came from Arabia to trade in the markets. With their sacks of gold strapped to their waists, they seemed wealthy and the boy often wondered how they accumulated so much.

The man wiped his forehead with his sleeve and turned to the boy, staring at him for a moment. A fresh bead of sweat crept down from his head cover and stopped at the wrinkles on his face. Each crease in the dark skin told a story of an experienced life.

"What are you running from?" he finally asked, pointing out the boy's rolled bedding strapped around his back. He spoke Latin with a strong accent and the boy guessed he traveled to Rome frequently to trade. Most of the foreigners had translators but many who came to the region learned to speak the language.

Felix shrugged and waved his hand toward the sea.

The man could see the boy was unable to speak but continued to stare and Felix shifted uncomfortably, pretending not to notice.

He has never seen a mute before. Perhaps he thinks I can fly, too.

"You know changing your location will not change your situation," the man said. Now he was intruding and Felix wanted to get up and walk away.

What does he know about my situation!?

He pulled on the collar of his tunic as if to straighten it like he often did when he grew angry or frustrated.

The man looked him up and down and spoke again. "I see many like you," he said. "They're running somewhere they think will get them a better life, only to face again what they once left behind."

The boy rose and started down the dock but the man grabbed his arm and looked him dead in the eye. His black eyes peered into the boy's soul. Felix's heart raced and a shiver jolted down his spine. He thought about the blade he had hidden in his bedding.

"You don't speak and you don't look like you are in much of a hurry to get somewhere, but for some reason I was drawn to you," the man said. "As sure as God is in heaven, you will listen to what I am going to say! I don't like to help vagabonds like you, wandering aimlessly. I have lived with people who are no longer here on earth who would gladly trade places with you!"

The man spoke in a low voice, almost as if he was ashamed to be speaking to the boy, and his scraggly beard danced with the motion of his lips.

The boy couldn't understand why the man was so annoyed—and why he bothered to come over to him in the first place. He had been minding his own business and hadn't been in anyone's way.

And how did he know I am running away?

The man spoke again, this time releasing his strong grip on the boy's arm. "I believe in omens," he said, "and always listen when my heart speaks. You are causing me delay. I have a large stock of fine garments loaded on that ship that I am bringing to the markets of Jerusalem for the Passover festival."

The boy had heard of the Jews and the trouble they caused for the Roman troops in the Judean region. He'd always imagined them as a wild people refusing the influence of a civil and industrious Roman Empire, so Jerusalem wasn't a place he wanted to go.

The man continued, "Several of my ships have been attacked in these waters by pirates. Roman ships only protect us for part of the way. I need someone who can stay on the watch through the nights."

Felix was puzzled.

People had always treated him as if he was a ghost wandering the streets and went to great lengths to avoid him. The "Mute Boy" made people uncomfortable when they had to communicate with him.

And now this Arab had approached *him* and had righteously accused him of what had been running through his mind these last few months on the hill. He'd been feeling sorry for himself, angry at the gods, angry at the world, angry at himself, blaming them all and now running from it all. It was clear the man did not think much of him but for some reason was offering him a job; Felix was not about to turn away an opportunity like this.

He nodded in agreement.

"Good, the ship is ready," the man said as he stood up. "My name is Haziq," he said, heading for the ship without looking at the boy.

Chapter 3. "Words spoken set life in motion"

The ships the boy had seen before were plain and built with the sole purpose of transporting goods. Haziq's, although still being used for transport, was elegant. Her masts stretched tall into the sky and the wood-work around the cabin and railings had been hand-carved with designs tracing through the dark wood.

principles allowed me to make the changes in my life I desired. I wanted to be wealthy. I wanted to be different from the men in my town who all lived their miserable lives following each other like the sheep they were tending.

"My problem was that I had a mind like they did. I thought like they did and I behaved like they did," the man stopped and looked up at the sky littered with stars.

It was dark out over the water as they traveled through the night and the wind continued to bounce the torch light over Haziq's face. The boy could see he was deep in thought and waited patiently, gazing around the ship.

A few crew men huddled around a torch at the bow, sharing stories of their own. The wind drowned out their voices and only the occasional laughter carried over to the stern where the two sat.

Felix's job required him to stay awake all night and then go to sleep at sunrise. If he saw any boat approaching, he was to sound the alarm and light the rest of the torches on the perimeter of the ship to illuminate all sides. He had walked the entire deck to see where each torch was and counted each one.

He'd placed his sword under the bedding of goat skins that he laid out on top of the roof and pulled the handle out, just enough to grab it quickly if he were to see any pirates. Every time he glanced at it, he was reminded of his reason for being on the ship and his heart beat faster. He hoped he would never need to use it.

Finally Haziq broke the silence.

"Some men are able to earn a lot of gold, some are able to discover their reason for existing, and some learn to be happy in their humble existence. Most will never have all three. If you truly want to gain wealth, wisdom and love, you must learn the principles and make them a part of who you are," he said.

Haziq again turned and stared at the boy, "Understand this. Never have I uttered these words to a man in all the days of my life. But I no longer can keep them in. By hoarding them, I have performed a massive disservice to the world. It is time the world takes upon itself the responsibility of its choices instead of blaming external circumstances for its failures. These principles must become a part of your very flesh, your mind, and they must make up the fabric of your soul."

"First," he continued, "remove all doubt and murderous self-destruction in the way you think and speak to yourself. Before all else, before you have any success, the first principle you must learn is this: *Words spoken set your life in motion.*"

The man leaned over and tapped the boy on the front of the forehead with his finger. "In here, you build your life and in here, you destroy it. It is your choice how your life unfolds."

The man watched as Felix struggled to understand. Up to this point, as hard as it was to accept his fate, life had been pretty simple. You work for everything you have, you gain a little and lose a little, and if you are lucky enough to earn more, you save. It didn't matter what you said or believed, the gods dealt with you as they pleased.

All Felix knew was that his luck ran out shortly after birth. If he couldn't speak to anyone else, what did the way he spoke to himself matter!?

"The universe echoes what you tell it. That is how God created it," Haziq continued, "You are here because that is what your heart requested most. Even if that is not what you wanted, it's what you asked for."

"Take an olive tree for example…"

The boy turned his head quickly and looked at the man; he had heard this comparison before. "An olive tree is barren for many years before it produces fruit, but does it believe it has failed?" Haziq asked. "Does it ever worry about what will become of its life? Does it tell itself that it will never amount to anything?

"It does not. It continues to grow, soaking up as much sun as it is given. It spreads its roots wide burying them in the soil, drinking in the water and energy from the earth. It never once considers itself to have failed, spring after spring it lives in faith that the time will come. It was created with a purpose—simply to be an olive tree."

"You boy," he went on, "You have given up on your roots. You have stopped asking the sun for its rays. You have stopped asking the earth for its water. Instead you speak lies to yourself. You told yourself the lies of others until you believed them. You told yourself every reason for why you *aren't* capable and you quit telling yourself why you *are*.

"Those people saw a mute and called you worthless. And you agreed with them."

The boy's mind flashed on many memories. Despite

his frustration at not being able to speak as a child, he'd not seen himself as different. His dreams and desires were not hindered by his disability and he never gave it a second thought when he first began to seek work. It was only when the others began to tell him he was different that he began to believe it.

Haziq stood up slowly and lowered himself down the side of the cabin. He made his way down the stairs to where others were already sleeping. Felix assumed he was retiring for the night but a few minutes later he reemerged carrying something wrapped in a cloth.

He climbed back up and sat next to the boy. Unwrapping the cloth, he pulled out a strange object. It was rectangular in shape, about the size of a large man's hand. The inside was made of paper cut into square pieces and stacked neatly. The outside was covered with animal skin and the whole thing was banded together by twine on the left side.

It looked like the paper used in scrolls. The boy knew paper was made of shredded pieces of wood glued together, pressed, flattened, humidified, and then connected to more sheets into a long scroll. He had seen the entire process when he had wandered into the shop where it was being made and the men working allowed him to stay. It was difficult to make and only the wealthy people could afford it as an option to chiseling stone or scribing onto dried animal hide like they'd done for so long before.

Haziq handed it to the boy. Felix took it and opened the thick cover of animal skin. He had never seen

much from Haziq as long as the man was willing to speak.

He began to write again. He would write a declaration to himself that had as much authority as the guards carried. He'd write out each principle as the man shared it and this way he would remember it.

"

Declaration #1: Words spoken set life in motion.

I will listen diligently to every word my mind tells me and I will interrupt it. I will judge it with the seriousness I would the most heinous crime. Every thought that is destructive and speaks against what I seek —will be cast out as if it was a disease of my mind.

I must silence any evil that comes from my mind as the universe is listening. It is listening and waiting to take action with the same force that moves mountains and with the same winds which dash waves onto the rocks. The same breath which taught the sun to burn with violence and the moon to cool the night is waiting for my voice and, until now, I have only robbed myself with my words.

When my mind speaks death, I will speak life and I will out-yell the words spoken against me until the voice in my mind becomes an unstoppable force, now speaking for me.

Soon the two voices will speak in unison and two will become one again. I will speak life because words spoken set my life in motion.

Chapter 4.

"Live with the end in mind"

The sun hung high above his head and his tired eyes burned but the boy was in no hurry to get to sleep.

He opened his book and read what he wrote in the night under the light of his torch. For the last few years, he'd listened to what people had to say to him and about him. Their voices had suffocated him and the voice inside his own head had joined the chorus.

Every time he'd think of success he'd get a reminder of his disability. A reminder of his parents leaving him as a child. A reminder that nothing he had ever tried worked in his favor. A reminder that he was always a step lower than everyone else. That his life served no purpose.

Can I really teach my mind a new way of thinking?

Haziq estimated it would be weeks before they landed in Caesarea and from there it was a few days' walk to

Jerusalem. But they would first stop on the island of Crete, at the city of Phoenix, for a few days before continuing to Caesarea.

The boy spent as much time as he could next to the man. Any time Haziq came up on deck, the boy rushed to his side.

When the weather turned and the rain grew heavy, they would move the cargo that was piled in the middle of the ship down the stairs to the storage below and then, when it cleared, back up to the deck. The ship was too heavily loaded to store it anywhere else. Haziq's books, fine garments and robes, and anything that was not water tight also needed to be protected. Felix moved quicker than everybody else, running up and down the stairs.

He enjoyed the tough work and was growing stronger because of it. The sweat streaming down his face and the energy that rushed through him made him feel like he was earning his spot on the ship and the meals the man provided for him.

Despite the harshness of his initial words, the man now treated the boy like any other crew member and he was grateful for that. He worked harder than he ever had in his life, not wanting to prove Haziq right. He would not be another waste of a life that should have been given to someone else.

Every day at sunrise, when most of the crew was already up, the boy retreated to the level below and tried to sleep on a cot. Most days he'd only manage a few hours thanks to the noise of the crew, the sea and the rocking of the ship. A few times he ran to the railing and vomited over the side. While some of the crew laughed, his humiliation was short lived as other seasick sailors inevitably joined him at the railing.

The crew kept track of the distance and the days but the boy had lost count after the third night. All of the days began to blend together and staying up all night only made things more confusing.

***

One cold night, he pulled his tunic tighter as he made his way up the ladder to his post. He spread his bedding, leaned back on the mast, and covered his legs with a goat skin that Haziq had given him. He had only the one tunic since he left Rome. Earlier in the day he washed it on the deck and waited naked in the sun as it dried. Haziq offered him clothing but he would not take it. He felt embarrassed to take anything more from the man who had given him so much.

The moon hid behind scattered clouds, making it especially dark, so he moved the torch behind him. Its bright light kept him from seeing into the distance but it provided him some warmth. He stared out at the dancing waves, hypnotized, and thought about the crew.

The men all had their own path that led them here. Some worked for Haziq, and had been sailing since their youth, some were here for the first time, but each still had a mind of his own. Each man must have had a dream—something they were working toward.

But most of them behave the same.

Haziq was wealthy, the rest seemed to be no different

from each other. He thought about his conversations with the man; "Each man has an equal opportunity to find the extraordinary life," Haziq had said.

But these men did not seem to have found theirs.

Was it because they have not learned the principles Haziq spoke of? Was he sharing them with others? Maybe they learned about them but did not follow them. Would he be able to learn and apply them to his life if so many had clearly failed to? He leaned his head back and closed his eyes.

They must not know of them.

Lulled by the ambiance of the crackling torch, the sound of waves repeatedly bullied by the hull of the ship, and lack of sleep, Felix's eyes grew heavy.

***

The entire ship suddenly jerked violently and the boy nearly flew off of his perch. He had fallen asleep on his post and, completely disoriented, jumped to his feet.

The boy froze when he finally looked up. A ship had rammed into theirs and now was positioned directly alongside. A rusty hook sailed over and latched itself onto the side of the rail.

"Pirates!" his mind screamed. Now he was able to move. He lunged for his sword and grabbed the torch, leaping from the top of the cabin roof and tumbling on to the deck. The torch flew from his hand but he held the sword tight and began slamming it on the side of a metal drum to alert the others.

A few men who were sitting in the cabin had felt the

jolt and came running and shouting. A second hook secured itself on the railing.

Soon the entire ship was awake and the rest of the men scrambled from below. Felix picked up the burning torch off of the deck and ran towards the next one to light it but before he could reach it, a man leapt over the railing from the other ship. The boy swung his torch mid stride as hard as he could and smashed it on the pirate's face. A shower of sparks rained down and the man stumbled backwards with a scream. The boy's heart pounded in his chest and the blood rushed to his head with the steady beat of a drum. He raised his sword high above his head ready to bring it down on the man—and suddenly everything went black.

Minutes later, he woke, head throbbing, lying on the deck with his hands and feet tied firmly with a rope. Men were yelling in a language he could not understand as he looked around. All of the crew, the captain, and Haziq were on their knees in rows along the deck with their hands tied behind their back.

The pirates did not look as he had imagined. He'd always thought them to be organized and skilled sailors but instead they were shabby men with big beards and uncut hair who looked more like unruly farmers with knives.

These were the men the Roman ships captured and dragged back to the city for trial and execution. These were the men who died painfully on the crosses he guarded. He'd heard tales of how Crete was full of pirates. They must be close to their destination.

Pushing his head against the deck, he managed to get himself up to his knees. One of the pirates shouted orders to the others as they cut the sacks and barrels being hauled up from below and loaded what they liked onto their ship. Every crew man from Haziq's ship was silent. Some were bleeding but, thankfully, as he conducted a mental count, no one was missing.

The shouting man who appeared to be the leader saw the boy get up on his knees and rushed towards him. Felix could not control the shaking of his body.

The pirate crouched in front of the boy. Grabbing him by his curly hair, he put a blade to Felix's throat. He began shouting in his language, repeatedly asking a question. Felix shook his head, not understanding. The blade dug into Felix's skin and he could feel the blood trickle down his chest. The pirate shouted again and the boy still could not answer. He looked up and their eyes met. The man stared at the boy for what seemed like a lifetime.

His sun-weathered face and untamed beard did not hide the deep scar that traveled up the side of his head.

This is it, the boy thought to himself as he stared death in the face.

Suddenly the blade dropped from his throat. The man stood up and walked toward his ship still looking back at Felix. He shouted an order to the rest of the pirates who grabbed the hooks and leaped back over the railing. As abruptly as they had appeared, they vanished into the dark. The boy fell to his stomach, again, nearly losing consciousness.

A few of the men broke loose and began untying the others. Haziq dropped to his knee and untied the boy.

"Are you alright?" he asked, "You took a club to the back of the head... I thought you were dead! That was brave what you did. They came upon us fast. Did you not see them?" His words were quick, but gentle.

Most of Haziq's goods were gone because the boy had fallen asleep. Felix was stunned to see the man looked more relieved than angry.

As he shook his head, he felt a sharp pain. He reached back and felt a large lump on the back of his head. The last thing he remembered was raising his sword above the pirate and he wondered if he really would have struck the man if he hadn't been knocked down.

What did the pirate see in the boy's eyes that stopped him from killing him!? Felix was so close to the end, but instead, his life was spared. Why? For what?

As Haziq helped him to his feet his legs were still shaking. They began to gather things strewn all over the deck and take an inventory of what was left. There had only been 11 pirates but with their surprise attack and the crew not having any military training, they overtook the ship with ease. As uninjured crew members tended to the wounded, the boy sat down again in a daze.

Clear skies to the east permitted the rising sun to light the undersides of the clouds, turning them a fiery red.

Using water he'd pulled from the sea in a bucket, the boy rinsed the back of his head and throat where the blade had dug in.

He found Haziq sitting on a barrel at the stern lighting his pipe with a hot coal. The boy sat down next to him and stared at the deck, head and eyes down. It had been his fault the pirates boarded with barely a warning. If he hadn't fallen asleep, this wouldn't have happened.

"Their ship is much faster than mine," the man said, smoke billowing as he spoke. "We had no chance to get away and they would still have caught up to us." It was as if he knew what the boy was thinking.

"They took everything except for my books. Perhaps they left my books because to a wise man, an empty book is a fresh start but to a fool, an empty book looks like too much work," he mocked. They continued to stare out at the horizon where the clouds and the sea met, the darkest spot in the sky.

"In Phoenix, we will report the incident to the officials, but we will continue to Jerusalem. I will bring my books to the markets of the world. This was another omen for me; I must continue. The goods I was bringing on this trip were the last of my purchased stock. I have gathered more than enough gold in my lifetime. My stables are many, my houses are filled with workers, my fields produce abundantly and my soul has drunk its fill from the pleasures of life."

"All things must come to an end and a new life cannot begin without the old one passing away." Haziq glanced at the boy and he knew the man was speaking about him.

"Men are foolish in that they take each day as if it is owed to them. They say, 'Tomorrow we will begin,' but tomorrow is only expected by fools. They make plans for a great future and they speak of it with dreamy eyes and yet they do nothing to arrive there. Men can be likened to a cow in the pasture, it eats what is in front of it with its head down and it is happy. But at the edge of the field, the farmer stands with an ax, ready to butcher it."

He took a long drag from his pipe. They sat facing the back of the ship, heading east in the direction of the sun as it rose over the horizon directly behind them, lighting up the darkness as if to let it know its time was up.

"We fear death because deep down we know that *we have not yet lived*. Time is a cunning liar—it deceives us by consistently raising the sun in the morning and bringing out the moon at night. We believe we will always have another day. But the universe warns us by the wrinkles on our face and the aches of our bones. Time will soon run out.

"Tonight, I did not fear death. I only feared that I may not have given to this world as much as I have taken from it. I feared that I have only used the principles taught to me for selfish gain."

He grabbed the boy's shoulder: "I fear I may not be given another chance if I continue to bury the wisdom given to me. One day my master will return and will ask of me what I have done with what was granted to me. Until now, I have kept it for myself.

"One must always *live with the end in mind*. He must remember his days are numbered or else he will fall victim to the lie. If he is to live his purpose and create the life he desires, he must see himself at the end of his days and from that perspective, be intentional about creating that life today.

"I have lived with this principle all my life and today I am reminded, that I *too,* have forgotten to live with the end in mind."

The boy went to his cot, but this time, the sleep did not descend as it had earlier that night. He reached for the book, turned to the second page, and wrote at the top. *"Live with the end in mind."*

He thought about the pirate who held the blade to his throat. It wasn't evil or anger that he saw in the pirate's eyes; it was desperation. He was looking at yet another man who failed to work for his desires and accepted what came easy, like the cow in Haziq's parable. This man had failed to live with the end in mind. A life like his would surely put him on the cross.

Felix once had a clear vision of what his life would look like, but that dream had died with the general's words and he was destined to become a beggar. In his mind, he'd been dealt a bad hand and his future was set in stone. Until now.

"

Declaration #2: Live with the end in mind.

I will live with the end in mind.

I will evaluate where I am today and this will reveal where my end will be.

The road I am currently on has only one destination. If I am not pleased with the destination, I must take another road and if I don't, I must accept my fate. I cannot and will not simply wish for change while I continue to walk in the wrong direction.

My future will not magically change. If I wish to change my destination I must first peer through the glass of time to my last day. I must decide how I want this day to be and I must decide what I want people to say about me. And what will they say about me? Will the world mourn or will it continue without a hiccup in the day? Did I live? Did my life serve a purpose? Was my life ordinary... or was it extraordinary?

I will live with the end in mind and, if I do, I will not stray. When I am lost and weary I will stop and look ahead. I will renew my strength and continue to walk the road ahead.

Yesterday's failures cannot stop me today as long as I live with the end in mind.

And when death comes finally knocking on my door, I'll gladly open and invite it in, for I'll know that I have truly lived.

I must live with the end in mind.

Chapter 5.

"In all things, be filled with gratitude"

The boy knew Haziq did not fear death and that his only concern was that his life serve a purpose in the time he had left. Very little seemed to bother him and this intrigued Felix.

Haziq spoke a lot of one God, his "Master." The boy made an extra effort to listen when the man spoke of this, setting down whatever he was working on.

Back home, people worshipped many gods in temples built for each of them. The boy was never interested in joining them. He saw people's belief in a certain god as a crutch, a temporary one. When life was in their favor, they worshiped and when the luck ran out, they cursed their gods.

They had always told him the gods kept the gift of speech from him. He felt like he had no need to thank them or curse them for it because they had done as they pleased. That was enough for him to decide they didn't need anything from him.

Haziq's relationship with his God was different. The man prayed and gave thanks before every meal. He prayed as he got up in the morning and as he retired at night. He gave thanks after they were attacked and he gave thanks for the goods he lost. Nothing seemed to shake him. It was as if he was living on another plane than everybody else around him.

"He sees what we do here," Haziq told Felix. "But He does not wish harm on any of us. It is us men who have caused the world pain. We rob and kill each other for material substance that He made available to all. We need simply to follow the principles given to us and we can receive freely—but instead we lack faith, we grasp at these material things because we think in lack. Thinking in lack creates lack and thinking in abundance creates abundance."

The boy loved the wisdom with which the man spoke. He'd never spent much time around a man older than himself and he wondered if this is what having a father felt like. All his life, so many questions had kept the boy up at night and he never had anyone to ask about them before.

Why do people have family, a home to live in, and still carry a look of sadness about their face?

Why do people complain and work at jobs they hate, and still do nothing to change?

What is everyone afraid of?

"To prosper," Haziq continued, "we must work hand

in hand with the things He gives us and with what happens to us. Without Him we cannot succeed. All of nature, even the rocks, respond to His whisper."

Again Haziq spoke in a parable: "All seeds need the same three ingredients to grow—sun, dirt, and water—but they produce fruit that varies in color, shape, and taste. In order for a farmer to reap a harvest, he must raise the seed to the sky and give thanks for the harvest the seed is to bring, in faith that what he gives thanks for will come to pass. It is God who infuses the magical power to spring forth a harvest. Without His breath the seed will not produce."

When the man turned to lock eyes with the boy, Felix knew it was time to listen very carefully so he could remember the words later. "You must learn to give thanks for all things in your life, boy," Haziq said. "For the great and the small, for the good and the bad, for the past and the future, for your life and your death. When you wish for a thing, you need only to give thanks for it as if you already have it and it will come to pass."

Haziq's voice grew louder, "Even evil men prosper when they learn the principle of gratitude. When you give thanks for the health you do not yet have, the universe responds with health. When you give thanks for the wealth you do not yet have, the universe responds with wealth.

"One day humans will discover that gratitude changes the inside of our minds and bodies. *In all things, be filled with gratitude.*"

Never in his life had Felix given thanks to the skies,

the universe, the gods of his people, and most certainly not to Haziq's God.

But if the man was right, what reason did God possibly have for not giving the boy the ability to speak?

How could he thank God for what had been a thorn in his side and kept him from doing anything worthwhile with his life? Why had he been given a life with no voice, no family, and no parents?

These questions were Felix's daily spoonful of bitterness. He compared himself to other boys and rarely saw anyone who had things worse than he did. After all, his decision to give up his life in Rome, leave the girl and abandon his plans was no fault of his own. It was his miserable circumstances that prevented him from any success.

But the boy had noticed that most men complained no matter their circumstances. He heard it on the hill from the other guards, he heard it in the orphanage, and he heard it in conversations at the market. No one seemed to have the money or home or woman they wanted.

It would anger him to hear it because he would give anything to trade places with most of them. Maybe Haziq was right. Maybe man's fault is that, he believes everyone else is better off.

Would he still find things to complain about if he could speak? If he had parents and a family and a normal life, would there really be anything else he would desire? He would often see beggars in the street missing arms or legs. Some were blind and some were deaf, but these were visible disabilities—his was not.

When they saw him, maybe they wished to trade places with him. Perhaps to them he was the thankless grumbler engulfed in his own misery. He walked by them tall and able on his feet, carrying produce with his two hands, avoiding carts and tables with the sight from his eyes.

Haziq was right once again. The boy had much to be grateful for.

***

"Crete!" a crewman yelled, startling the boy from his nap on the roof. They had made it to the island. It had been weeks since they had seen dry land—and the enormous island looming in the evening sky with the mountains towering in the distance felt like a miracle. The rocky hills and dried grass showed no sign of life until the ship sailed farther along the shore. Finally Felix spotted the city tucked away beneath the mountain.

As they drew closer, he saw torches bordering the waters. Phoenix was a small city and the harbor sat in an inlet with hills protecting both sides from the winds. The ship slowly entered the harbor, stirring up a flock of screeching seagulls, and they docked for the evening. Some of the men left the ship and headed into the town, but Haziq, the boy, and a few others stayed aboard for the night. They would be up early the next day.

The boy sat for a while looking at the peaceful town lit by torches along the docks and the streets, still burning as dusk turned to night. The gulls had quieted and the sound of the wooden ship, creaking as it rocked on the waves, took over. A couple of fishermen floated into the harbor on a small boat and tied it to the docks in front of the ship.

The name *"Masir"* was painted on the side of Haziq's ship and he'd explained that it meant "the path" in Arabic. How fitting it was. This journey had carried Felix far from home but it was a path he had willingly taken.

He had something else to be thankful for. They had made it here alive and in a few days would embark again for their final destination.

Felix exhaled deeply as if he had been holding his breath the entire trip. Every night he tried to push the thoughts of danger away as they came, but after the pirate attack, the entire crew remained tense and the worry in the air was contagious.

He looked up. In the clear sky, the stars sparkled like millions of tiny candles. He stretched his hand towards them and spoke in his mind.

Thank you.

He grabbed his book and opened it to the third page.

"

Declaration #3: In all things, be filled with gratitude.

In all things, I will be grateful.

With my legs I walk. With my hands I hold. With my eyes I see. With my ears I hear. With my mind I think. With my heart I live. With my lungs I breathe.

If I start to complain I will count my blessings. I will write them on my sleeve and I will never forget them. When I wake in the morning I will raise my hands and say, "Thank you! I am alive another day."

If I lack I need only to ask. I will ask for a thing as if it were already in my possession and I will say "Thank you."

In my sorrow I will seek for things to be grateful for and in my joy I will give thanks.

In all things, I will be grateful.

Chapter 6.

"Each day, give of yourself more than you ever have before"

"Up boy, it is time," Haziq shook Felix awake. Two crew men with bloodshot eyes and the smell of strong drink still on their breath, joined as they headed down the ramp to the docks.

They walked through the narrow streets—already alive and bustling as people rushed about their business and the boy wondered if they even slept. Men hauled fishnets to the docks and prepared their boats for the day. Donkey carts heavily loaded with sacks of grain were unloaded from delivery ships and then sold to other ships that needed to restock.

Despite the newness of the experience, Felix was tired—the man had pulled him from a deep sleep. He wanted to be back in his cot on the ship.

He'd only dozed a few hours the night before. The

excitement of the first part of their voyage caught up to him and he realized how tense he had been the entire trip. From the beginning he was anxious, being surrounded by people and constantly worrying about attack had taken their toll on him. If pirates struck again, he might not be so lucky.

Back at the orphanage, he had been left alone except for meal time when all the children gathered around long tables. He knew that most of the others assumed he was deaf as well as mute and never bothered to speak with him; he didn't bother to correct them. As he got older— he worked alone and that was best.

On the ship, however, things were different. Few of the men had known each other prior to the trip but, a few days in, all were well acquainted. The boy had been tossed into the middle of life on board the *Masir*.

Suddenly he was surrounded by grown men, working side by side and sharing meals together. The sudden change had been difficult at first. He tried to distance himself, knowing that sooner or later they would speak to him and when they realized he was different, they would reject him.

Beyond his nightly perch, he had nowhere to hide and was forced into the daily routine on the ship.

Within the last few weeks of their trip, Felix had become a man. He was now treated like one and surely felt like one. He jumped to the assistance of anyone before they could even ask for help. He outworked the crew and soon he was the one everyone sought when they were either shifting cargo or working in the heat below deck.

Never before had he been given the chance to display his strength and he used any opportunity he could to show he had earned his place onboard. He even surprised the otherwise stoic and monotone Haziq. The man's eyebrows nearly sprung to his hair-line when he saw the boy emerge from a crawl space of the ship, red-faced and drenched in sweat. A crew man had been assigned to tar the bottom of the ship below the walkways and the boy beat him to the job.

He was as strong and able as every man on board and now he had proved it.

***

The foursome spent the entire morning carting supplies from town to the docks and up the ramp to the vessel. Haziq wanted to replace the most urgent orders that were lost in the attack. He left the boy and the two crew men to the work and wandered off through the city, making deals and arguing with the local sellers.

It was midday when they finally carried Haziq's many purchases onto the ship. They had the rest of the evening to themselves. The boy set off to the east, passing through town and continuing on the dirt road along the shore, watching the waves crash against the rocks, spraying him with a salty mist. He came to a bend and began climbing the rocky bluff.

At the top, he dangled his feet over the edge and stared out into the ocean. It was peaceful up here and reminded him of the hills he often climbed overlooking the city back at home. He spent many days up there dreaming of riches.

Felix looked down at his hands covered in blisters from the morning's work, carrying the sacks and bundles wrapped with rough string that dug into his palms. They looked like the hands of a man.

He smiled.

If Haziq can teach me to earn even a small amount of money, one day I will put this effort into my own fields. I can plant rows and rows of olive trees and tend to the land, I can till it and rid it of all rocks. I can plant and care for them on my own."

The boy took a deep breath and closed his eyes. The fresh breeze filled his lungs and this time instead of anxiety and fear, his heart beat faster from his thoughts of the future. Maybe he really could become what he once dreamed he could be. He enjoyed the feeling —the feeling of being alive, being valuable to the world. Now he understood. His dream had never left; it was he who had quit on it.

Back on the *Masir* the boy was rolling out his bedding for the night when one of the crew men called him from the dock, "Boy, get up and come with us!"

They'd all been invited to the home of the market vendor from whom Haziq had purchased wine.

It took nearly an hour to walk to the estate and they finally arrived at the top of a mountain overlooking the city. They passed through a large gate in a wall that was about the height of the boy, and continued following the road to the entrance of the house. On each side, Italian cypress trees lined the road and near the entrance, torches burned to light the way. The house looked like a palace.

By the time they arrived, the rest of the men were already seated around a large table on the back patio, feasting. Piled on large platters were meats, vegetables and fruits. There were fish and cuts of lamb; a large vine of grapes, spilling over its tray; and silver vessels filled with wine. As he walked in, the boy marveled at the high ceilings and thick pillars that made up the architecture of the home.

When he was purchasing wine, Haziq had showed the host his new way of making books and they had made a deal. The host, a great salesman as well, had ordered a large number of the empty books. Haziq would employ more help to prepare them and ship them back to Phoenix in the near months.

The man had sold an entire order before he even had enough help to fill it. The boy shook his hand with a smile to congratulate him. The two were seated at the end of the table across from the host as Haziq explained everything in a low voice.

The rest of the crew carried on loudly, sharing stories and drinking the wine that never stopped flowing. Several servants stood around the table through the night, refilling any cup that came close to being dry.

The few times Felix had drunk, he purchased the cheapest skins he could afford, but this wine was different. It was delicious and it was strong.

This must be what the emperor drinks.

With each sip, he could feel the liquid flow down his throat and chest with a warm burn until it settled in his belly.

It didn't take long for him to feel it in his head. Everyone talked and, laughed, and the boy laughed with them. To his surprise, the wealthy man and Haziq chuckled along with the men's crude jokes and even contributed a few. The group's drunken voices carried far off into the hills.

The table was set on the bricks outside and only lattice work woven with grape vines separated them from the open sky. The boy saw the stars through the leaves, shining bright as the night before. A servant tended the fire crackling in the pit next to them, which made their shadows dance on the hills.

When the conversations eventually died down, Haziq raised his cup.

"God was watching over us on our trip here," he said. "And he will watch over us as we continue our journey. I lost a large investment in the attack, but we were spared our lives and that is of most value."

All of the men nodded and raised theirs as well.

He continued, "A drink to life… and a drink to Felix for smashing a torch on that poor chap's face!" The men burst into laughter and cheered as Haziq roughly slapped the boy on the back, nearly knocking the wine from his hand.

Felix smiled and the drinking resumed loudly as each man attempted to out-yell the next with his recollection of the story.

The men thanked the owner of the home for his hospitality and slowly made their way back to the ship. The man and the boy walked in the rear.

"You have learned a principle on this trip that even I would never be able to teach you," the man said. "I have never seen someone as eager for work as you are. You have earned your spot on the ship."

He went on: "Most men will wait for an opportunity to show up before they begin working, but the truth is the work needs to be put in long before the opportunity shows up. Few will ever learn that Lady Opportunity chooses wisely who she visits. Opportunity always has a way of finding those who are busy and already doing the work.

"Some men tell the stove to give them heat and then they will add wood. But they must first put in wood before the stove will provide heat. I created the books and opportunity came knocking today. I would not have made a sale if my idea was only an idea in the mind. My trip could well have been in vain after losing everything in the attack. Now, I have made a friendship that is already more profitable than what my original sales would have been.

"Men must learn to *each day, give of themselves more than they ever have before*. If you continue to approach each day the way you have on this journey, you will prosper in all things."

Haziq stopped and looked at the sky. Thick clouds

began to hide the stars. "Looks like trouble in the morning. Get your sleep, boy," he said.

On the ship, the boy lit a torch and opened his book to the fourth page.

"

Declaration #4: Each day, give of yourself more than you ever have before.

Each day, I will give of myself more than I ever have before.

Each day, I will rise before the sun has finished its sleep. As it rises, it will find me about my business and it will shine on my labor.

I will not sit idle and seek Lady Opportunity from the seat of my ass for she sees the lazy man and walks past his home. I will labor and she will draw near to me. I will not rush her, for by faith, I know that she is making her way to me.

Each day, I will give of myself more than I ever have before.

I will not concern myself with the work or pay of others and I will not compare the difficulty of my labor to theirs. I will do the things that others avoid today so that tomorrow I will receive the things others merely dream of. I will do more than I am paid to do and soon I will be paid for more than I do.

I will not judge my labor, big or small, for I will always give my greatest effort.

Each day, I will give of myself more than I ever have before.

Chapter 7. "Blame no one but yourself"

A vicious rain beat the deck, causing a cold river of water to flow over the boy's bare feet before it ran towards the railing and over the edge. It sounded like the stampede of a thousand horses as it hit the wood and the crew fought to secure the sails being whipped by the violent wind.

He was glad he had paid attention to how the crew managed the sails on the calm days. The captain was screaming orders and it would have been impossible to learn in these conditions.

He stood, holding the railing and breathing heavily.

The ship was finally set on track and there was nothing he could do besides weather the storm.

The salty spray pelted his face each time the ship dipped into a large wave and he held on tightly.

They were further than he had ever been from Rome and the distance grew all the more as the ship turned south for Caesarea.

He wished the girl could see him. Now, he was a real sailor and she would surely be impressed. She only knew the frustrated and lonely boy who was different from all of the others and she pitied him. He enjoyed her company but had grown more ashamed as the years went by and he grew older.

His cheeks flushed red as the memories of each encounter played through his mind. She was with him every time he was turned away by potential employers. She would speak with the merchants, shop keepers, and officials in the government buildings who looked him up and down as he stood, uncomfortably pulling at the collar of his tunic. It was humiliating and after a few attempts he no longer tried.

One day she even found work for him. She came back from the market and told him about a man who needed his help, but the boy refused out of pride. Now, he looked back in regret, thinking how quickly he had given up when she had tried so hard to help.

The declarations flashed through his mind. If only he knew then what he believed now, things would have been different.

As he looked out over the waves, pounding the ship endlessly, he suddenly became aware of his white-knuckle grasp on the railing. It wasn't the storm making him tense, it was his frustration with his past. Confined in this small space day after day, there was nothing he could do to distract himself from his thoughts.

He blamed the gods. He blamed his mother for leaving him as an infant. He blamed the Roman army for banning him. He blamed everybody else for keeping him from his dream.

In his short time on the ship, he had proved he was equal to any other man but why couldn't others have seen that earlier? Why had it taken him leaving everything he had ever known to prove himself worthy? If they had given him more opportunities and weren't so ignorant, perhaps he could have led a normal life.

That night, Felix had an odd dream.

In the dream, he was surrounded by a large crowd and held his book close to his heart. The crowd was impatiently waiting for him to speak but a familiar horror came over him as he made an attempt to open his mouth but could not move it. He tried again and again but, one by one, the crowd dispersed until only one man stood alone in front of the boy. The man had tangled hair and a thick beard, and his bare feet were coated in dust from the road. He stepped closer and stopped directly before the boy. He stared into his eyes for a long moment and the boy stared back, his terror beginning to fade.

Though he appeared to be a poor wanderer, the man's dark eyes searched the boy's soul. This look of deep compassion turned the boy's tears to sobs. In his dream, the boy felt this man understood his pain. Then the man, still not saying a word, stretched out his hand towards the boy's mouth. The hot coal he held touched the boy's lips. Felix stumbled backwards from the burn. "Who are you!?" he shouted.

***

"Patrol!" the crew man shouted, jerking the boy awake.

As he jumped out of his cot, he kept thinking about the dream. Maybe the man was his father. Others in the orphanage had spoken about dreams where they saw their parents even though they had never known them, but the boy had never experienced it himself. And he'd had many dreams in which he tried to speak but this one was so clear and disturbing. What did it mean?

He climbed to the top deck and looked out where the crew was gathered. A large roman patrol ship, twice the size of the *Masir,* had pulled up beside them. The Roman officer shouted and Felix and the rest of the crew quickly scrambled to pull the sail and stop the ship.

The boy exhaled, pleased to see the emperor's flag waving high in the wind and pleased to see it wasn't another attack.

The Roman ship was now directly beside theirs and just like the pirates, the soldiers threw hooks over the railing and fastened the ships side by side. An officer led 10 soldiers down the ramp they'd set down from the taller ship. The patrols stopped and searched every ship they came across as the threat of pirates and rebels spread throughout the seas.

Haziq had told the boy this would likely happen.

The officer did not entertain Haziq's small talk and ordered the ship to be searched. These men did not waste time. The boy noticed the battle scars that covered the Roman ship—as if large chunks had been ripped from its hull. The men also appeared to have fought often, with deep cuts and dents across their chest plates and worn-out uniforms.

They looked exhausted with their tired eyes and certainly had no care to be friendly as they marched about the ship, opening every satchel and barrel.

These are real soldiers, Felix thought as his memory darted back to the men back at home who were fat and pale, and their uniforms were shiny new.

If I had been able to join, I would be out here with these men, protecting Rome instead of splurging on the spoils.

He remembered the man who hit him on the hill only a short time ago and was disgusted at the memory.

A soldier came up from the bottom deck and spoke to the officer in a low voice. The officer looked around and with a shout, ordered the crew to line up along the railing.

"What is the matter?" Haziq asked, but again, he was ignored. The soldiers pushed the crew into a row and stood guard. The boy's heart dropped to his stomach.

The soldier who approached the officer was holding

the boy's pack. And his sword.

After examining the sword, the officer stepped in front of the crew and stared each one down. The boy's throat was dry and he tried hard to swallow. He had seen the execution of deserters. How could he explain why he was in possession of the sword so that the officer would believe him?

Finally, the general turned to Haziq, "Who does this blade belong to?" he demanded. The man stared at the double-edged blade and its ridged leather handle without responding.

"There is a deserter on this ship," the general spoke again and he looked at the boy. Felix was the only beardless man on board and certainly did not look like a common sailor. All of the men on board were rough and dark—and most of them looked to be from the southern part of the world like Haziq. The boy was the only light-skinned Roman citizen.

How stupid of me not to return it!

Haziq darted a quick look at Felix and their eyes met. Just as soon as the boy was about to step out, the man spoke up, "It is mine!" he said, "It was given to me as a gift in Rome."

The general stepped up in front of the boy, ignoring Haziq.

"What is your name?" he asked. The boy nervously motioned to his mouth.

"He is unable to speak," one of the crew men spoke up. The general's weary eyes studied the boy as the dyed-red horse mane on the crest of his helmet waved in the wind. After a moment, he handed the sword to Haziq, still looking at Felix.

"It's a shame. A strong boy like you would have made a great soldier," he said. He turned sharply and the long red cape fluttered from his wide shoulders as he marched in the direction of his ship.

The patrol continued their search of the ship and when they hadn't found what they were looking for, headed back to their own.

Once again, the *Masir* caught a southeast wind and sailed on its way.

"Did you run from the army?" Haziq said, pushing a paper towards the boy with a frown.

They had finished their meal and now sat in the cabin. The boy wrote on the paper: *The sword came from my work as a guard. I never returned it. They did not allow me to join the army. They said I would create a weak spot. That's what I have been my whole life, just a weak spot in society.*

Haziq did not react as he read it.

He pulled out a wineskin with the markings of the rich man from Phoenix on it and the boy guessed he had stocked up on the quality wine. He poured himself a cup and filled a second for Felix.

They drank in silence as the room grew dark. Only the glow from the candle on the wall of the cabin gave light.

The man began: "When a man blames another or a thing for his failures, he loses the ability to gain control of his life. As long as he continues to blame, his life will remain the same. If he wishes to change his circumstance, he must first acknowledge his participation in it and only then will he have the clarity to begin a transformation. Until then, he is blind to the path that leads to change; for how can he mend a broken thing when he does not recognize it is broken?

"And if indeed the circumstance he is in is no fault of his own, what else can he do but seek the way through? If this ship is sinking and the crew does not wish to perish, they must accept the reality of the sinking ship and make the decision to repair it or abandon it.

"If the crew begins to blame each other, they will certainly die. If the crew begins to blame the ship, they will certainly die. If the crew blames the water pouring into the ship, they will certainly die. They must find a way to survive without pointing in blame." Again, the man spoke directly at the boy.

"You must own your *kara*," the man swore in Arabic. The boy had heard this word many times on the ship and by now he knew that it meant "shit."

"Whether you are telling me the truth or not, it does not matter. The only thing that matters now is that you stop blaming everyone for your place in this world. It is your path to walk and not the fault of any circumstance or person. See it, accept it, and proceed. Only then will you be able to see the clear path to an extraordinary life," Haziq paused, pulled out his pipe and lit it with the candle.

Felix started arguing in his own mind. Everyone had treated him so unfairly for so long, how could he be at fault? He couldn't speak!

"Take a look at the men on this ship," the man continued. "They would never in a thousand centuries admit their own failures if I were to ask them. Any one of these men is capable of achieving anything they desire and most of them surely would rather be at home with their families, yet they are here working day and night, staring out at this endless sea.

"But if I ask them why they have not created a plan that will give them freedom from their laborious struggle, they will give me a long list of people and circumstances that are to blame. They will blame God, they will blame their luck, they will blame Lady Opportunity for not presenting herself, they will even blame each other, but never will they point their fingers at the real problem which lies in them.

"You, boy, don't have to be like them. Put away the old thinking that everything happens *to* you and see that things happen *for* you. It is simply the way you respond to each circumstance that determines your success or your failure. Just as soon as you acknowledge that it is only you who stands in the way of the extraordinary life, you will leave the ordinary behind. Blame only postpones progress.

"When I was still a young man," Haziq continued as he stood up, "I watched many days pass by as I pointed my fingers in every direction but my own. I was the master of excuses. With this, the only thing I truly mastered was a remarkable ability to find blame in everything.

"We can justify our limitations or we can learn to

break out of them."

Felix had in fact found a way to be useful on the ship. Could he have found a way to be prosperous back home if he hadn't blamed his circumstance for his failures?

Haziq began descending to the lower deck but the boy grabbed his book and headed for the roof.

He opened his book to the fifth blank page and began to write.

"

Declaration #5: Blame no one but yourself.

If my pride, anger, or laziness blind me from opportunity, I will blame no one but myself.

If I am working until my old age and my hands and feet are tired, I will blame no one but myself.

If my satchel does not ring with the sound of gold, I will blame no one but myself.

If my house is not built and my fields are not bringing a harvest, I will blame no one but myself.

If my relationships are failing, I will blame no one but myself.

When I am challenged with difficulty and I refuse to face it, I will blame no one but myself.

As I examine my life and I see things that bring me shame, I will blame no one but myself.

Only I have the ability to create my happiness and if it has eluded me, I will blame no one but myself.

For my successes, I give myself credit, but if I fail and have the urge to blame, I will blame no one but myself.

Chapter 8.

"Develop a burning desire"

When the boy first stepped on board the ship, his only goal was to create as much distance between himself and Rome as possible.

The loneliness he felt on that last day on the hill was more than he could handle. His life had lost all flavor and he had found himself numb, going about his days in a trance. The days began to blend together.

It was better for him to disappear than to have the girl see him fail yet again, or worse, depress into a beggar. The pain of knowing that he would probably never see her again was dulled by his need for change. Maybe... just maybe... there was a chance things would turn for him but it wasn't going to happen in Rome.

A few days earlier, the man had spoken of another principle and he had not rushed to write this one down as he had previously done.

"If it doesn't consume your mind than your desire is not strong enough," the man had said. "It is not enough to simply wish for a thing and hope that someday it will show up at your door. You must hurt for it. You must feel empty without it and you must want it so much that you can see it every time you close your eyes.

"If it burns in your belly and it is the first thing you think about when you awake, the last thing you see when your head hits the pillow, then it is a burning desire. If it truly is burning in your heart, all of the universe will conspire to bring it and lay it at your feet, there is no way that it cannot, it is a law of this world."

It was one he understood long ago. But his vision of a land in the hills, covered with olive trees—the thing that Haziq called a *burning desire*—had dwindled to a measly flame, eventually growing cold in a stream of smoke like an extinguished candle. The boy had once felt what having a burning desire was like. This one came as no surprise to him.

The man had spoken of a time when his own dreams were only an idle wish. As he continued to wish, they remained a wish and it was only when they turned from a wish to a flame, and the flame to a burning desire, did he finally discover success.

Felix thought back on his visions of an olive orchard on the hill to the north of the city and the house he would have that overlooked the trees and opened to the view of Rome. Everything he did was fueled by his intent to achieve it. But as the opposition stacked up against him, the dream began to fade.

"Without a vision and a burning desire to see it manifest, a man will do no great thing because he will quit at the first difficulty he is faced with," it was as if Haziq was reading his mind again.

"A burning desire to see it manifest will push him through any obstacle, it will give him a faith that few have ever seen and no matter what lies ahead of him, he will persist."

The man continued, "I wanted to become rich and give my family the freedom that I wished for myself. I dreamed often about how great it would be and yet I did nothing to increase my sales and the gold I earned. I was earning enough and I had just enough.

"Only when the vision of my dream began to visit me more frequently, until I was no longer able to sleep, did I begin to seek a better way. It gave me a hunger like no other and it lifted me through struggles that I never would have had the courage to fight before."

The ship dipped up and down as it pressed on over the large swells and the two held on to the railing as Haziq spoke.

"It was only the strength of my desire that has carried me thus far. You must create a vision for yourself that soon turns into a ghost, haunting you day and night until you see it come to pass. All great men of this world and those that will come after, are driven by desires that pushed them to limits far surpassing their own God-given skill or abilities.

"If you have a burning desire for a thing, you will put

yourself on an equal plain of any man, no matter what you lack. The universe will find a way to bring it to you; you must only want it enough. This is a prerequisite of experiencing the extraordinary life."

That evening the boy rearranged the sacks of grain piled on the deck and plopped himself in between. They protected him from the constant wind and provided a comfortable cushion.

He thought about what he desired most, and once again, allowed the image of the olive groves to enter his mind. There was nothing in this world that he wanted more than to spend his days in his own orchard, cultivating the land and planting the seeds, running the dirt through his fingers, caring for the trees, and gathering the harvest.

He let himself imagine.

As he planted each seed he would speak to it and he would tell it to be patient. He would tell it that its time would come and no matter how long it took, there would come a day that it would bring to this world its fruit in abundance. He would have the thickest grove producing more fruit than any trees in the land. They would take up an entire hill, they would cover the entire mount and his olives would be requested from all over the world. He would have a ship like the *Masir* to transport his olives throughout the lands.

The boy stood in the breeze with his eyes closed feeling a renewed hope wash over him. He hadn't written this principle in his book because he was wrestling with fear. He was afraid to let the flame burn like before. What would happen to him if he failed yet again? But slowly, he began to submit to the idea, allowing it in.

I don't know how, I don't know where, and I don't know when," he thought to himself, *"but whatever it takes, I will work until I am standing in my own grove.*

He found Haziq reading in the cabin and stood above him. He slid the paper across the table. The man looked at it for a moment before he read it aloud: *"I have recorded all of the principles you speak of thus far and I have a desire that will never fade again. You once spoke of a time that you realized yours. If you are willing to continue teaching, I am willing to continue learning."*

A rare smile formed on the man's face. "If you have been recording what I have been teaching," he said, "then you have already done more than most men will ever do when it comes time to pull their heads out of their own rear end! Many know these principles but few will ever act on them."

"Be diligent in making them a part of your very being. We will see if it truly is a burning desire that you carry in your heart," Haziq said as he patted the boy's chest with his palm.

That day, the boy continued to hold the picture in his mind and he became aware of one thing; every time he pictured his land, his house and the rows and rows of olive trees, the girl was always there.

If what I desire must come to me, then Licinia will be brought to me."

He did not know how this was possible. Maybe she

would already be married to someone else? But he pushed those thoughts away quickly, there was no room for a clear picture of his desire when doubt crept in. One day he would see her again.

"

Declaration #6: Develop a burning desire.

I must have a burning desire for a thing if I wish to achieve it.

A wish is simply a wish and it will remain a wish until it fades. If I desire to turn my wish to a thing I possess, I must have a desire that burns for that thing.

As I rise in the morning and lay my head to rest at night, I will create a picture in my mind's eye of that which I wish for. I will feel it, I will taste it, I will hear it, and I will speak to it until my desire becomes my reality.

I will fan the measly flame of that idea until it bursts into a roaring fire that turns the dark days of my life to brightness and the bright days brighter.

When it is but a tiny flame, I will speak not of my desire so that others will not extinguish it with their words. Only when it burns strongly and no great sea can quench it, will I no longer fear what others know of it.

Any man who speaks to me may not know of my desire but they will see in my eyes a flame that shines deep from within my soul and they will not wish to stand in the way of that flame, which is my desire.

Thousands upon thousands that have come before me and more that will follow after, will wish for a thing, but few will understand the magnetic power of a burning desire.

Michael V. Ivanov

Many wish for a thing, yet few will achieve it. For in order to receive a thing, I must have a burning desire for that thing.

I must have a burning desire for a thing if I wish to achieve it.

Chapter 9.

"You must take action"

The seagulls screeched as they circled the skies waiting to swoop down on the fish laid out along the docks. Large ships had docked and hundreds of sailors, slaves, and locals milled around, loading and unloading. Men hurried to move the smaller boats out of the way as Haziq's ship was guided in.

Man-made walls extended into the water, closing in the entire harbor. Only a small opening, large enough for ships to come through, gave access to the *Masir*.

Felix used the ropes of the sails to pull himself up and latch his feet around the mast. He climbed, bear-hugging the wood post until he was near the top. He could see the massive coliseum, with its chiseled pillars, standing proudly among the smaller buildings.

As Haziq explained, Caesarea was an insignificant city

salesmen."

They walked past a merchant selling sandals and Haziq stopped.

"I was no wiser than any of these men. Many of them dream big, but most won't ever leave the comfort of these familiar streets. The only difference between them and me is that I chose to act.

"This is a thing you must learn. You either take action or join the masses—those who merely dream but never get to where they want to go."

Haziq turned to the seller and began speaking in his language. As they spoke, the boy quickly reached into the pack on his side where he carried his book. Standing in the middle of the crowded street, he opened it to the next blank page.

At the top he wrote, *"I must take action."*

He did not want to forget this principle. Later, he would find time away from the overwhelming sights and sounds of the city to write.

The man thrust a pair of new sandals into the boy's chest and the boy looked at him with surprise.

"For you," he said. "We have a long walk ahead of us in a few days and those don't look like they will last through the evening," he pointed at the boy's feet and the tips of his toes that reached out slightly past the edge of his worn-out sandals. The man had taken care of him through the entire journey and Felix was desperate to find a way to repay him.

I will not take the full payment of my wages when he offers. I will start giving back everything I earn for all that he has provided for me until I no longer am in debt to him.

He hated taking things from the man. Back at the orphanage, people brought clothing, sandals, food, and many other things for the children and he had always hung around at the back as the others ripped through the supplies.

They walked through the sleeping city until they reached a large stable where Haziq had arranged the rental of a camel and a donkey to carry supplies and pull the cart.

When the two arrived back at the ship with the animals, the crew was already up and had packed the cart. Everything was ready for the journey. Only Haziq and the boy would make the trek and the rest were to stay with the ship and await their return.

They headed through the city until they came to the south gate and continued down the dark road. The cart wheels rattling and the donkey hoofs clip-clopping on the large flat stones were the only sounds in the dark as they traveled away from the city. Soon, the stones ended and the much-used road continued as dirt.

They walked in silence for hours as the moon hid and the sky began to brighten. The boy wore a large scarf over his usual tunic and he pulled it tighter around his chest. His arms were bare but they had gotten used to the cold on the ship as he slept—he would only cover his body to keep warm.

He thought about what Haziq said back at the market, about those people who only talked about doing great things and never took action.

The only action I have been quick to take is to quit. When faced with difficulty, I sure don't hesitate to act—I just go the opposite way. Felix's thoughts grew more sarcastically as they walked.

From now on, any opportunity that comes my way, no matter the amount of fear I will face, I will do everything I can to act on it.

***

The sun sat high above their heads as the road began to wind upwards towards the jagged mountains. To either side, the valley stretched far, and the dried grass created a sea of yellow, rolling in the wind. The rocky path made for a difficult walk. The boy's thighs burned as they continued into the hills and with every bend, the road seemed to get steeper. He was used to walking every day back home, but the relentless uphill climb soon wore on him.

To his left, the cliff dropped sharply and he looked down to see how long the fall would be if someone were to get close enough to the edge. He wrapped his head with the shoulder scarf to protect himself from the heat of the sun. Haziq remained silent as they pressed forward and conversation only came when they stopped to eat. They breathed hard and every once in a while, the man motivated the camel as if it understood him.

"Just a little more now, old friend," he said.

"Camels will quit when they've had enough; the ass will walk until it drops dead," he said. The boy walked behind the cart and pushed it when the road turned steep to help take the load off of the poor animal.

They had just come around a large bend in the road when Haziq whistled and yanked the donkey's strap to a stop. A naked man was lying on the side of the road.

They ran to the motionless body. Blood ran from his head and face and large bruises covered his entire body. From the sunburn on his skin, it looked like he might have been there for hours. Only a meager breath proved him to be alive.

Haziq retrieved a wine skin and a jar of oil from the cart and knelt next to the man. The boy lifted the man's head as Haziq poured water into his mouth and the man choked out a heavy breath. His eyes remained swollen shut and he let out a whimper as they attempted to sit him up. Haziq tore pieces of cloth that covered the supplies in the wagon and after pouring the wine and oil into the wounds, began wrapping each bleeding cut.

"Bandits," he said, "The hills are full of them. No one should ever travel alone here. We will take him with us and see if we can get him help in the next village."

They shifted the goods in the cart and stretched out the cover. Carefully laying the man down, they set out on their way. The boy took off his head scarf and laid it over the man's face as they walked. An uneasy feeling nagged him as they hiked and the boy glanced to the sides and up to the ridges of the hills, hoping not to spot what he searched for.

He walked in the rear and watched the limp body being tossed by the cart as the wheels hit rocks and dips simple beauty of life together!?"

A few hours later, Felix sank into the layers of thick wool, finding joy in the simple beauty of his bed. It was paradise compared to his cot on the ship. Under the candlelight, he pulled out his book and opened to the seventh page where he had written in the market.

"

Declaration #7: You must take action.

I must not only speak, I must take action.

No man acquires gold by merely speaking of it.

No man achieves greatness by simply talking of it.

No man fulfills his purpose by only thinking of it.

In all things that I wish to achieve, great or small, I must take action.

I am not what I say; I am what I do. It is my actions that will reveal who I am.

Opportunity presents itself often and only those that take action will reap the benefits of its riches.

The world is full of men who speak of a thing or teach a thing but it is taking action towards that thing that makes it real. Withholding action only makes the thing an idea, and the world, although seemingly built on ideas, was in fact built on ideas followed by action.

If I claim to want a thing, I must not sit with arms folded, I must act with arms swinging.

I must not merely speak; I must take action.

Chapter 10. "Always persist"

Legs aching from the previous day's journey, Felix wondered if he could get through yet another full day of walking. While he prayed they would no longer face difficult terrain, he was determined not be the first to quit for a break.

They strapped the cart to the donkey again and Felix went around to fetch the camel in the stable behind the inn. It was a gentle animal but he cautiously secured the leather strap around its jaw imitating what Haziq had done. The boy had seen camels bite and despite the humor he found in it, it looked painful.

He gazed at the layers of clean, dry hay in the stable, and the indentation where the camel had been lying. Even the camel must have had a great sleep. He imagined what it would be like to lie back down in the hay the camel had warmed, and enjoy a few more hours of sweet slumber.

The innkeeper was already up, tending to the fire in the dining hall as Haziq approached him. Handing over a few coins, Haziq asked him to take care of the injured man until he was well. On the return trip to Caesarea, he would stop and pay whatever the innkeeper felt was a fair price. The boy admired Haziq's care for this complete stranger—just as he had shown care to this man, he had also taken the boy, a runaway mute, under his own wing for the past month.

Much of the road had been desert but every few miles, where there was even a tiny stream, palm trees grew thick and curved upwards to the sky. The grass was greener than he had ever seen and he pulled his sandals off every time they stopped at an oasis for the animals to drink. He dunked his face in the cold water and pushed his bare feet into the grass, feeling it between his toes.

I bet olive trees grow better in this land than any other.

***

Felix could see the enormous wall towering in the distance. It had been torn down and rebuilt time after time and the distinct color of brick revealed the history of each layer. He spotted the massive temple, dedicated to the God of the Jews by The Great King, emerging among the sea of smaller clay buildings.

The endless squeak of the cart wheels finally ceased as they arrived at an inn just outside of the city wall. It was late afternoon and Haziq paid for their stay, ready to retire from the long journey, but curiosity had overtaken the boy. He kept turning over his shoulders to gaze at the walls as they unpacked the animals, fed, and watered them. As soon as they were done, he headed for the city.

Jerusalem was far from anything that resembled Rome. The soldiers posted on street corners were the only indication of Roman control.

It was very much alive in the evening as caravans, carts, donkeys, and camels entered the gates with him as he walked. The setting sun encouraged weary travelers who hurried to find lodging. Most of the travelers undoubtedly were coming from distant journeys, with dirty feet, and restless animals.

Felix knew that it was here, long ago, that Haziq had begun his career as a salesman. "Nobody knew me in Jerusalem so when my poor salesman skills led to rejection here, it was much easier to swallow the shame," the man had said.

Men of the temple strolled the streets majestically with straight backs and attire that looked strange to the boy. Their colorful robes, reaching the ground, needed to be pulled up frequently from the dusty streets. Tall hats perched on their heads with gold strings looping around, bouncing with each step. They reminded him of how the women dressed back home and wondered why anyone would agree to such a look.

He ran up the steps to the wall on the east side of the city to where he could see the entire land far past the

their entire lives, and he, a mute, would be trying to sell to *them*.

If he did not try, it would surely prove the failure he had always been. But if he sold the book, it would be his greatest victory yet.

He headed for the marketplace.

As he approached, the sellers stared at him, waiting for him to speak. Each time, he would hand them the book and then the paper. All of them waved him off. Nobody had a need for the book. Some would flip through the blank pages and some even seemed intrigued, but then they would shake their head no.

With each rejection, his anxiety grew. The boy fiddled with the collar of his tunic. He wanted to go back to the inn but then he'd hear Haziq's rough accent lecturing him, telling him there was always a buyer and he only needed to persist.

Late in the afternoon, the boy was hungry, tired, and hadn't made a sale. His back ached; this seemed to happen often when he endured the stress of interacting with people. There were so many uses for the book but nobody seemed to see that. He himself had marveled at the idea and immediately had found a great use in it for his declarations. Most of the merchants had already gone home; the rest were clearing out their displays.

The boy headed for the inn with his head down.

How is it that even with a great idea like this I cannot sell? He began to blame himself.

If I could just explain to them all the uses, surely I could sell one.

On his way back to the inn, he decided to tell the man that he was no longer going to try. Without the ability to speak, there was no hope for him as a salesman.

Haziq burst into laughter when the boy, with red cheeks and head hung in shame, handed him the book. "You have learned the first thing about selling," he said. "Everyone thinks they have a great product until it doesn't sell. Selling is no easy task and that is why so few succeed in accumulating large amounts of gold.

"When I started selling, I thought it was going to be easy. I would present my product, they would pay me, and I would move on to the next customer. I borrowed enough money to buy five robes and with the profit, I would pay back what I borrowed, leaving me with enough to buy more and repeat this simple process as I thought.

"But it did not work like I planned. My prices were 'too high,' my robes were 'poor quality,' and no one seemed to need one. I tried to sell to every merchant in my town and they all laughed. I even knocked on every villager's door. I was the son of a poor man and when they would see me approach, they mocked me. So I packed my belongings and traveled here to Jerusalem. Surely, I would sell in a place where nobody knew me or my family. They would see me as another merchant. But I was wrong. Still nobody bought from me and after a few days, I traded my robes for just enough food to last me my journey back home."

They sat on the roof of the inn, under a tent cover strung on wood poles overhead to protect them from the evening sun. Haziq drew from his pipe. It was hard for the boy to believe that this wise man who had so much was once so poor and defeated.

"When I made it back to my town I went to work in the fields for a year before I tried selling again. Then, I told myself that I would sell one robe and that was all. One, just to prove to myself that I wasn't a failure. I had to put a stop to the embarrassment that ate at me every day. So I began again and soon realized what I had lacked. The location, the people, the merchandise—none of these were my problem. My problem was my inability to persist when things became difficult.

"Soon, I sold my first robe, the next week after that, I sold six, and then I added more garments and larger quantities."

The next morning, the boy rose before Haziq. He carefully tore the last page away from his book. On it he wrote a new pitch. If the merchants couldn't think of a need for a book, he would show them.

He wrote the price at the bottom and made a list of all the ways one could use a book:

-Sellers could use it to track inventory and sales.

-Men of the temple could use it to copy their laws into it, in a much simpler way than the traditional scrolls.

-Roman centurions and generals could use it to keep account of their duties.

-Old men could use it to write their tales and legends that, up until now, were only stored in their minds.

-Teachers could use it in schools when giving lessons to children.

-They could use a book any way they used a scroll but far more efficiently and less expensively.

It was still dark when he finished writing. He folded the sheet into his pouch and set out for the city. He was more confident now and when he passed by the gates, nodded to the few soldiers who paced back and forth trying to stay warm in the cold morning air. He would be the first in the markets once the merchants began to roll in and set up their stands and he would help them. Even if they purchased his book only because he helped them, he would accept the victory.

The streets were still empty. He climbed the long steps to the wall and his heart was racing by the time he got to the top. He sat on the edge facing the city, breathing heavily. The temple of the Jewish God was illuminated by torches and the courtyard stretched wide and far.

He looked toward the hill he had planned to explore that day, but decided he was not going to leave the walls of the city until he sold the book. Persistence was one principle the boy had failed to live out in his life, always quitting at any sign of resistance. He was determined not to give up, no matter how many times he was turned away.

The merchants began arriving from the outskirts of the city as shop owners brought out their wares. The boy approached a man lugging carpets from inside his home. Felix quickly grabbed one of the carpets to help the man stretch it across a rope. The man nodded and asked a question in Hebrew. The boy motioned to his mouth as he usually did. The Jew nodded and smiled. He continued to help the man bring the rest of his stock out to the street for display.

After they had finished, the boy reached into his pouch and pulled the book out with his paper and handed it to him. The man flipped through the empty book and then pointed down an alley.

Unsure of what the man was pointing to, Felix headed in that direction.

In the dark alley, he saw a table scattered with scrolls. More scrolls leaned against the walls and were piled high on the shelves. Stairs led up to a door that faced the alley from the second story. Underneath the steps, he saw a patio under large beams that supported the house above. It looked as if it had been converted from a stable into a work space. As he approached an old man sitting in a chair, scanning a scroll, the man looked up at the boy.

Deep wrinkles bore into the old man's wizened face and a fringe of white hair surrounded his balding scalp. His long beard nearly reached the table he was working on.

The boy realized immediately that this man transcribed copies of written material per order and felt foolish that he had not thought of approaching men like this before.

He noticed the man was copying a military letter that had the emperor's stamp on it. This man would need the book more than anyone! He nodded apologetically as the old man looked up from his work. The boy was clearly interrupting and the impatient stare made him want to turn around and leave.

Instead, he stretched out the book with his paper and the man took it from him. He did not read the paper but instead leafed through the book and raised his bushy white brows. When Felix remained silent, he looked down at the paper. Opening the satchel on his waist, the old man handed him the coins for the book.

Slightly startled, the boy took the coins and put them in his pouch, smiling. As he was turning to leave, the man grabbed his arm.

"This was made with great quality... do you have more?" he asked in Latin. His wrinkly hand gently floated down the cover of the book as he spoke. The boy had written the pitch in Latin and now realized that many of the merchants he planned on approaching might not have even understood like this man did. He was in a land where they spoke Hebrew and Haziq's note had been written in Hebrew. The carpet seller must have pointed him here simply because his book was empty.

The boy pointed at where he had written Haziq's name on the paper.

"If this is your price," the old man said, "I will certainly take more of these as soon as you have them. I know others who will find this greatly useful. This month alone, I have many orders to transcribe."

Realizing the boy was unable to speak, he wrote on the back of the paper: "*Ephraim of Jerusalem: 500 books*." The boy's eyes widened as he saw the amount, but he managed to straighten up and shake the man's hand as firm as he could. He had watched Haziq do this many times before—it's what great salesmen did. He folded the paper into his pouch and stepped out into the alley. Struggling to contain his excitement as he walked, he paced himself in case the man was still watching and held onto his pouch firmly with both hands, lest he lose the precious note inside.

As soon as he rounded the corner, he broke into a sprint and ran as hard as he could. His legs burned and a sharp pain pierced his side, screaming for him to stop, but he only pumped faster. When he reached the street that led back to the inn, he instead turned south. People stopped and watched him run by like a mad man, nearly knocking over a woman in his haste.

He slowed to a jog through the gate before ascending the road towards the hills he had previously spotted. As the road turned steeper, he began to walk and turned to see the city behind him and the wall he had sat on earlier that morning. He gasped for air but continued to walk, knowing he was going in the right direction.

As he drew closer, he spotted them. Olive trees! He turned from the road into the orchard and started to run again with his hands spread wide, letting the branches and leaves hit him in the palms and the smell of the fresh olives fill his nostrils.

He found a clearing and falling to the ground, began to weep.

For the first time in his life, he had found success in something he set out to do. He had sold a larger order of books than Haziq had with the wealthy man in Phoenix. And he had done it by himself, without Haziq's help! He had battled the fears like so many times before but this time he was not mercilessly beaten to his knees. This time… he was victorious.

The boy rolled over and sat up, double-breathing, as he tried to inhale more air, finally calming. As far as he could see past the city walls stretched palm trees, streams, and hills that rolled into the distance and, once again, he marveled at the beauty of this land. Even the bustling and crowded streets of Jerusalem seemed less intimidating after his triumph.

Drying his eyes and wiping his hands on his tunic, he stood up. He navigated through the rows of olive trees, making his way back to the road and to the inn.

Haziq would be proud. Not only because he had a large order to add to his previous one, but the boy had found a way to sell with his own approach.

Back at the inn, the boy noticed Haziq had not yet returned so he headed to the roof patio. He pulled out his book to the eighth blank page and began to write.

"

Declaration #8: Always persist.

A single drop of rain may not be noticed, but drop after drop, it drenches an entire land. Like the rain, I will persist.

A river carves its path into the canyon not by force, but by persistence. Like the river, I will persist.

For every door slammed shut in my face, I will knock on two more. I will persist.

Although I get weary, day by day, and the end seems nowhere in sight, I will persist.

If I lack skill and talent, I will persist and I will surpass those more talented and skilled than I.

The world is full of people with dreams but my dreams will not stay merely dreams because I will persist.

I may kick, I may scream, I may fail, and I may cry, but as long as I am still alive, I will persist.

When I try, the world may hold me down but when I continue to persist, they will step aside and watch me pass by.

I will not quit,

I will persist.

Chapter 11.

"You are a creature of habit"

Felix and Haziq entered the city for the evening to share a meal and after finding food that finally pleased the man's eye, a freshly grilled lamb, they sat down to eat.

"I was not surprised that you sold the book. I was not even surprised to see the large order. You have had a fire in your eyes these last few weeks and you are a different man compared to the scared boy I first met on the docks," Haziq said as he washed down the meat with a sip from the wine vessel. "That day you looked lost and I knew you were lost.

"All who lose sight of, or never find their purpose in the first place, carry a similar look," he said. "It is a dangerous state of mind. When the mind does not have a destination, it is like a large ship that leaves the harbor without a captain or a crew. It will end up on some beach, a derelict, if it ever leaves the harbor at all.

"You seem to have an idea of where you want to go

now or else you would never have followed me here to Jerusalem. If you were yet another vagabond being carried to and fro, whichever way the wind blew, you would have left as soon as we docked. I believe you want something greater and you are seeking something greater—and this is exactly where you need to be.

"The man who purchased from you saw the same thing I see in you. Everybody wants to be in business with one who refuses anything short of greatness for himself."

The boy took a bite as he listened to the man intently. It pleased him that the man noticed. Perhaps it was something that would help him make more sales, this fire in his eye.

"One thing you should know," the man continued. "Not all sales will come so quickly. You stayed persistent and you made your sale because you chose to try again even though you wanted to quit."

Haziq went on to describe how persistence creates habit and humans are creatures of habit: "God created our minds to work in an interesting way. Your mind sees the way you behave and the choices you make daily. In an attempt to make life easier, it creates habits of these choices. Soon, the simple choices you made daily have turned into a way of life, whether you're aware of it or not."

"Think about your sleeping habits for a moment," Haziq said.

"I have been waking you every morning while it is still dark out and you never fail to show your displeasure. I wake up earlier than most men because it is those who rise early that meet opportunity. You, on the other hand, love your sleep. When you sleep, you miss the knock of Lady Opportunity. And she is not rude. She will not interrupt your sleep."

A blush of shame colored Felix's cheeks.

"Create habits that power you through those days in which you do not feel like getting up," the man went on. "It's better to make a few small sales daily by being consistent in your approach than to make large sales less frequently through spontaneous emotions and behaviors. You will lose the willingness to continue when faced with a few failures but the habit of persistence will allow you to continue despite the results. You won't exceedingly celebrate your successes and you will never drop into depression from your failures. You will simply rise another day, and proceed."

They rose from the table and Haziq paid for the meal. Felix imagined a day when he would be able to pay for the man.

Haziq lit his pipe, and the pair walked silently to the inn. When they walked through the gate he spoke again. "Habits are a matter of great importance in all aspects of life, not only in the business of selling. Your life today reflects much of the habits you have created. Do not take this lightly."

As soon as the man woke him in the morning, the boy jumped to his feet. Sleep tempted him but he was determined to develop the habits of the man. Haziq had told him that he awoke at the same time every morning out of habit and he wanted to do the same. Over the past few days, the man had sold all of the goods he brought with him and today he planned to meet a merchant in the city to discuss an order of books.

Haziq had originally wanted to leave for Caesarea as soon as they sold everything but now, they would remain in the city for the Passover festival. Hundreds of merchants from all over the world would be attending and the man wanted to sell more books. He didn't need help on this particular morning and if the remaining books were not sold, the boy could try his luck again the next day.

Felix placed his own book into his pack and headed back to the hill. He wanted to go back to the spot between the olive trees and write.

He purchased a loaf of bread at a market cart and walked through the city. Jerusalem was getting more crowded as the days went by. As travelers flooded in for the annual celebration, Felix began to feel less like an outsider.

He thought about how the man had spoken so strongly about creating habits in order to be successful. He wanted to be wealthy and wise like Haziq, so he would need to do things the way the man did.

He would first focus on making a habit of each of the principles he had learned and written about from the man. If he mirrored the man's behaviors, he would surely be met with success.

"

Declaration #9: You are a creature of habit.

Wherever I am, I am there because of my habits.

Today, I still do things that hold me back and I do not do the things that will move me forward. But I am a creature of habit and I must learn that I can only do the things around which I have formed habit.

If I am not where I want to be then I must look at why this is so. If I am not where I want to be then my habits are to blame. If my habits are those of a lazy man, then I must settle for the pay of a lazy man. If my habits are those of a poor man, then I must settle for the life of a poor man.

I must learn the habits of the man I desire to be and if I succeed in forming these habits, then I will succeed indeed.

By forming habits around the things I need to do, I will do them even when I have no desire to.

My mind is a powerful and unstoppable force, waiting for my command. Whatever I have commanded of it, I will surely see.

I am… a creature of habit.

Chapter 12. "Love will set you free"

He was nestled between the olive roots at the edge of the hill, just before the rows dipped down steeply to the bottom of the mountain. Suddenly he became aware that someone was near him. He whipped his head around to see a man standing only a few feet away. The boy quickly rose, assuming he was in trouble.

This is probably the farmer, angry that I am in his field.

He'd finished writing in his book and had leaned back in the grass, closing his eyes.

He thought how different things would be if he returned home as the man he was now. Would the familiarity of his surroundings cause him to eventually drift back into the mindset he carried in Rome? Or would he be able to carry his new confidence and enthusiasm for life into his old routine?

No amount of gold was worth trading for the wisdom he had gained on this journey and even the thought of falling back into the shackles of old thinking frightened him.

He started to dream about the girl but quickly pushed that thought away. Her memory only brought a sadness that was, at times, unbearable.

"Shalom," the man said with a smile.

It was a Hebrew word the boy had heard many times in the city but he continued to stare, unsure of its meaning. The man paused before he spoke again, in Latin.

"I love it here too," he said, "This is where I come to get away from the chaos," he pointed to the city below.

The boy smiled and sat back down assuming the man would continue on his way. Instead, the man approached the edge of the hill and sat down beside him, gazing at the landscape before them. Not seeking a conversation he would soon prove he couldn't be a part of, he glanced at the stranger for a second and then back at the view.

Felix guessed this plain-dressed Jew was a local, trying to escape the influx of pilgrims flooding the city for the festival. The man looked at the boy and continued smiling. Though he felt uneasy, Felix noticed a kindness in the man's eyes.

Perhaps he feels sorry for me.

"They can be hard to tolerate," the man said, looking down at the city. "Each one lives so preoccupied with himself. So focused on his own well-being that he can't enjoy life directly around him."

He sat in silence for a moment, eyes not focused on anything in particular, before he continued, "Watching them go about their days is like watching an infant as it plays. It cannot possibly comprehend the miracle that is its life, but the father watches in joy and with a plan for its future.

"If they could for even a moment, fathom the love that envelops them, they would not be so anxious, so worried, so hungry for the future, to the point of surrendering the present. It is not what is around them, but what lives inside, that can bring happiness, purpose, and wealth. Simply understanding this would bring them peace.

"Is this not so?" He looked at the boy. Felix nodded in agreement but he wasn't quite sure he understood what the Jew was speaking of. What kind of love could take away fear and worry?

"There is far more to life than the food you put in your stomach, the clothes you hang on your body, the jingle of coins in your purse. Look at the birds, careless, in the care of God. How much more are people worth than birds!?

"Has anyone ever gained an hour of life by worrying? All this time and money wasted on appearance—do you think it makes that much difference?

"Notice the fields with wildflowers," the man waved an arm out over the vista. "They never primp or shop, but have you ever seen color and design quite like it? Even the greatest kings of the earth, in all their glory, have never dressed like these.

"If God gives such attention to the appearance of wildflowers—most of which will never be seen—don't you think he'll do his best for you? If they weren't so preoccupied with *getting,* they would be open to God's *giving.*

"What if they could see what God is doing right now, and not get worked up about what may or may not happen tomorrow? What if they could know that—God will help them deal with tomorrow's things, tomorrow.

"Instead they develop sicknesses, stresses, and anxiety. They live in fear. They create destructive habits and poisonous thoughts. They steal, envy, murder, and destroy each other."

The boy was puzzled about why this man had joined him and was spilling out his thoughts, but, the words were simple and full of wisdom. The Jew's plain words made the worries of man seem so minute.

Felix had lived a solitary life and everything he perceived and understood came from his own lonely experiences. Until he met Haziq, he viewed the world through his own pained perspective.

"They could earn any amount of gold they desired, achieve anything they put their minds to, and find the purpose to their existence by simply choosing love. If they lived a life deeply rooted in love, they would not be constrained because perfect love casts out fear. They would live in abundance of such wealth, it would flood their storehouses and they would not be able to contain it all."

The Jew picked up a twig and fiddled with it as he spoke.

"But those who pursue gold for the sake of possessing more, place a vail over their face. They become blind. Here begins the crawl through life, grasping at mere drips of joy, while true life and abundance has eluded them."

The man then looked at the boy, "Why do you not speak?" he asked.

Felix was startled—he had assumed the man already noticed that he was unable to speak and now his face turned bright red. He motioned to his mouth and touched his lips.

"Why do you not respond to me?" the man asked again.

Perhaps he is blind, How does he still not see?

In frustration, the boy motioned to his mouth again, in the way he had done all his life. People always seemed to understand, but this man was clearly not observant.

The man did not respond. He continued to stare at the boy but this time he was not waiting for a response. His eyes searched the boy's as if trying to glimpse his soul but the slight crinkles of the skin around them told another story. They carried a look of compassion and kindness. There was no smile on his face but the deep brown eyes seemed to conceal a smile and they looked familiar to the boy.

Only the sound of a soft wind rustling the leaves of his beloved olive trees made its presence known. The boy fidgeted with his collar and glanced away from the man's stare.

Suddenly he realized why this man looked familiar.

This was the man from the strange dream he had on the ship!

The boy's heart seized violently and began to pound in his chest. He was afraid the man could hear it.

Who is this man!? Does he know me? Maybe this was not coincidence and he followed me here!

"Do not be afraid," the Jew said. "Nothing is coincidence in the world of man. Everything that moves and breathes between heaven and earth is seen… and everything is immersed in the greatest love.

"There is no greater desire the creator has than to know and embrace all, especially those who cry out to him in their hearts. He cherishes those most." He continued to stare at the boy and a smile came over his rugged face.

"All of your tears, your dark and lonely nights, your pain and your anger have broken His heart into more pieces than they have yours. I can see it in your eyes, boy, you have carried your burden for a long time." The man spoke strangely but his words reached the boy's heart. Tears began to well in his eyes. He looked away to hide them.

If only this Jew really understood! Here's another well-wishing encouragement from someone who cannot possibly know how this feels.

The man reached up and ripped an olive leaf from the tree. He rubbed it between his fingers vigorously and rolled it into a ball. Stretching out his hand to the boy's face, he touched Felix's lips with the crushed leaf and as he did, he spoke loudly, *"I don't have much, but this I can give you. Be free from your muzzle, boy."*

The strong and familiar smell of the olive plant flooded his nostrils but as soon as the leaf touched his lips, a sharp pain shot through the boy's jaw and something popped in the back of his head like a cracking whip. A strange sensation filled his mouth, the constant flex of the muscles in his jaw released and his tongue fell loose.

The boy tried to stand up quickly but stumbled backwards and fell on his rear. "Who are you!?" he screamed. Only this time, the words were not in his head.

He had spoken.

***

Something had happened. Something had changed when the leaf touched his mouth. Was this man a witch doctor? The Jews practiced all sorts of strange rituals— was this a temple man!? Still in shock, he touched his mouth and jaw with his hands and moved them, making sounds with his lips and mouth. "WHOA!" he shouted, and the vibration of his voice rumbled through his chest and throat and came bursting out of his mouth.

He swung his arms wide and lunged at the man with an embrace, falling to his knees and nearly pulling the man down with him. He grasped onto the man's garment with both hands and buried his face into the man's shoulder, weeping.

Time passed and the boy still wept. It was as if he was ripped awake from a paralyzing nightmare and it finally released its hold on him.

Maybe it was no accident that he ended up here? He thought it was his failure that drove him here to this strange land and these strange people, but now he wondered if perhaps it was Haziq's God who called him here.

Finally he sat up and looked at the man who also had tears in his eyes.

"Are you a man who speaks to this creator you talk about?" he finally asked, "Does he know me? Did he send you to fix me!?" The movement of his tongue in his mouth was the same one he had attempted to replicate time and time again when he was a child but now, the vibration moved through his chest and throat as his voice came out. He continued to hold his throat, feeling the rumble transfer to his shaking hand.

"May I see him?" the boy exclaimed.

The Jew smiled. "Every time you look into the eyes of another, you are gazing into His. You need simply to look deep enough. He is always there. It is in the eyes of man where heaven and earth collide."

He pointed at the thick walls surrounding the city below, "You see, the walls separate the city from the rest of the land but it is still one kingdom. The city below can be likened to heaven and the land surrounding it as far as the eye can see represents this world. When your time is up, you will enter into the gates of the city and then you can meet Him. But don't be so anxious for the end—use the time you have been given to discover your life. You are in this world for a reason, aren't you?"

He embraced the boy and turned, beginning to walk away. Felix tried hard to make sense of it all as his mind continued to race. He grabbed the man's arm, "Sir! Thank you for what you have done for me!" he said in a shaky voice.

"People will search all of their lives for a mere glimpse of heaven but heaven is not where they seek it," the man said. "It is here, it has come down. Show the people a better way to live," he added with a smile.

"How do I do that!?" the boy exclaimed. For the first time in his life, he had a question he could actually ask someone. Now he couldn't be ignored! The man pointed at the boy's pouch and book on the ground which had fallen out.

"You're doing it right now. Teach them the principles you set out to understand for yourself. You are learning them with a hope of a better future, but what you have decided to declare over your own life, others must learn to do the same. They are the foundation one must build upon. With them one can gain gold. With them one can gain wisdom. With them one can find happiness," the bearded stranger said. "But the greatest use of them all, is that one can discover the elusive path to his own purpose, and find the extraordinary life.

"Just as you have been shown much love, do the same for them. It is no easy task. Many seek, few will find. You must not merely keep them for yourself. Gold will give you possessions, but *it is love that will set you free*," he turned and headed through the rows of trees.

"Where are you going!" the boy yelled, but the man turned into the trees and was gone from his sight.

On the roof of the inn, he paced in circles. Who was this Jew that had healed him!? He had embraced the boy when he cried and at that moment, had lifted the weight of his burden from his shoulders forever!

The boy opened his book to the tenth blank page, and through tears, began to write.

"

Declaration #10: Love will set you free.

My bitterness and my hate, my anger and frustrations, my envy and my disgust, my misfortunes and my lies, have chained my mind, but it is love that will set me free.

When they attack me with their words, I will remember that it is they who hurt inside, and I will teach them that it is love that sets them free.

If I am to succeed, I must first learn to love without greed. Whatever I set out to do, I will approach it with love and my love will empower me to succeed.

The world is broken and can only be fixed by one condition... It can be fixed with a love that is without condition.

I will love, because I now know that I am loved.

It is love that sets me free.

Chapter 13.

A treasure discovered

"Haziq!" The boy screamed from the roof as he heard the man approach. He dropped his book and ran down the stairs, through the inn and out to the street.

Haziq stood motionless, still holding onto the straps of the donkey. His brows were knitted tight, and his dark eyes fixed on the boy as he ran up. He was not certain if he had indeed heard the boy speak and had not moved a muscle the entire time it took Felix to get down to the street.

As they sat in silence on the roof of the inn, Haziq's pipe burned slowly but he never took a drag. The boy could see the man's eyes grow misty as they reflected the sun's dimming glow.

Throughout their journey, Felix had seen kindness,

forgiveness, and generosity, from Haziq. But he'd never shown emotion like this.

He brimmed with joy as Felix told him of his encounter. For once, it was the boy who spoke endlessly, pouring out his story to the man. He told the man everything from his childhood to their meeting on the docks. He told him of his final days in Rome that led to him running away. He spoke of the girl and of his job as a guard. He told him of the transformation that had taken place in him from all Haziq had taught, and how he had restored faith in himself, despite his limitations.

Haziq had many questions for the boy but he was particularly interested in the man from the mount. He pried for every detail. What did he look like? Was he a Jew? What did he say? Where did he come from? Did he say who he was?

When he spoke again, it was a soft mumble and the boy could hardly make out the words: "He may be the one. He may be the one they have spoken of."

The boy did not understand. Had Haziq heard of this man before? He told Haziq of his strange dream on the ship and how the Jew looked much like the one he saw in his dream. The man puffed on his pipe and continued to stare into the distance, the sun glowing red now as it was about to set.

"The prince of peace..." he whispered, "The prince of peace may have arrived."

***

The city was crawling with people as they navigated their way through the crowds. Haziq had asked the boy to lead him back to the transcriber who requested an order of books from the boy. He wanted to speak with the man and discuss the delivery.

The old transcriber held the boy's face by the chin. His leathery hand squeezed Felix's jaw and he whispered in Hebrew as he continued to examine the boy who'd experienced a miracle. They had told him of the Jew from the mount.

As the two men continued to talk, the boy sat on the steps and watched the people in the streets busy about their day.

Many were coming to the temple to pray and prepare for the Passover festival. He thought about the temples in Rome and how the people worshipped their gods there. He found it strange that despite these different gods, beliefs, and religions, the people here and in Rome were so much the same. They lived the same way and they all seemed to value the same things. The only difference he could see between a Jew, a Roman, and an Arab was that their faces looked different.

They all worked to provide for themselves and family, they stopped and laughed, gossiped, and spoke with friends, finding the little happiness in life and yet, they were longing for a deeper meaning to their lives, a higher purpose, as each one came to the temple, praying for his own problems, searching for answers.

What was the use, he thought, of living, believing, and behaving a certain way, yet having a life that was identical to everyone else's? Each person was entirely unique yet they seemed like sheep to him, following the plans and eventual failures of everyone else.

Did not all of them end up on the same bed of regret when it was time to leave this world? What was the use of conforming?

He couldn't be the only one with greater desires, greater dreams. All of these people must have dreams of their own. All of them must have hopes, wishes, and aspirations for a better life.

It must be a difficult thing, to let go of the comfort and safety of the ordinary life.

Perhaps this was why the Jew from the hill had asked him to teach the declarations he had been writing.

But he was only beginning to learn the principles for himself and he wrote only what applied to his own life and thoughts. Not everyone had the same problems he did. What could he teach to people who had a more difficult life than him? And he was so young. What could he teach to people who'd been on this earth a lot longer?

The idea frightened him and he could not think of a way he could do so even if he had the courage and knowledge to start such a thing, which he didn't. He thought again of his dream and how the crowd had dispersed as he was attempting to speak. That is what would happen if he tried. What could he say?

It was only in the last weeks of his journey that he'd begun thinking differently. If anyone could teach people these principles and the way to a better life, it would be Haziq.

He is the man for the task, not I!

As he sat on the steps, Haziq came out and called for him. He asked the boy to bring his book in and show it to the transcriber. They flipped through the pages that the boy had written and he stood back, fidgeting with his collar, hoping they would not read his declarations. Haziq wanted to show the man how the ink did not bleed through to the other side of the pages. The old man seemed to ignore Haziq however, and instead scanned through the writings without saying a word.

That evening, as the boy was preparing for sleep, he reached into his pouch and his heart dropped into his belly. He felt the few coins and the small jar of ink, along with his quill pen. His book... was gone! Had he left it at the transcriber's shop? Or did he drop it on the way home!?

He frantically ran into the night and traced the path they had taken back to the inn. As he walked through the city gate, a lone soldier stood near the entrance corking his wine skin when the boy approached.

"You are out past curfew, boy. What is your business?" the soldier asked as he stepped in front of Felix.

"I have lost a thing that is very dear to me sir. May I look for it?" Felix replied.

He glanced down the road past the soldier, wishing with every ounce of his being that he would spot what had become so important to him.

"Return to where you have come from," the soldier

replied. "We Romans are an enticing target to some people from these parts, especially an unarmed boy like yourself."

Felix was partially relieved: the soldier saw he was a Roman too. He still wore his tunic and had not taken the clothes Haziq had offered. This soldier may have reacted with much more hostility if he was dressed like an Arab or Jew.

But still he pleaded with the man, "I won't be long, sir!"

"Go home boy!" This time the soldier shouted and gripped the handle of his sword.

An idea entered the boy's mind making the blood thump in his ears. He had been faster than any boy at the orphanage and all his days exploring the hills in Rome had turned his leg muscles to iron. Surely he could out-run this man who was clothed in heavy chest armor and a helmet. He had left the inn barefoot and pouch-less. He needed to find the book now—if he waited until morning, it would be gone.

He quickly side-stepped the man and broke into a sprint.

"HALT!" the soldier shouted and chased after the boy.

The wind whistled in his ears and the adrenaline fueling his body continued to pound in his head. Two more soldiers came running in response to the shouts and Felix barreled into them as they appeared around a corner unexpectedly. All three came crashing to the ground.

The two soldiers lunged for the boy, but with a quick roll, he was off the ground and running again. He finally found the old transcriber's alley and ducked into the dark, away from the light of the torches.

He covered his mouth to silence his jagged breath as his chest heaved. He stood still until he no longer heard the shouts.

Hours passed as the boy sat in the alley. He could not search the streets anymore and it was too late to wake Ephraim. And if he went back to the inn, the soldiers would surely see him. He would have to wait until the light. The book had to be here in the transcriber's shop... he prayed it was.

Several stray dogs passed as he shivered in the cold. He thought about everything he had written in the book. He'd read his declarations daily and had memorized most of them. But the book had given him such comfort and security. Lying in bed at night, he would hold it to his chest. It was as if his very heart and mind were receiving their life from it, and now it was gone.

At dawn, Ephraim came down the steps from his house above and approached the door to the shop directly underneath his home. The boy hopped to his feet and approached him. The old man flinched in surprise and squinted his eyes as he peered at the boy. "What can I do for you so early this morning?" he asked.

"I lost my book last night... I hope that you may have seen it in your shop?" Felix nervously rubbed his elbow and his eyes were fixed on the man—who was in no hurry to respond.

"Come in," He finally replied, "I would like to speak with you if you have some time for an old man." He unlatched the door and the boy followed the man into the shop.

He waited as Ephraim lit candles on the walls, frantically scanning the room for the book. It was not here.

The shop smelled of ink and glue. The glue was used to connect scrolls together and the boy wondered what gave it the strong odor that stung his nostrils. The man swung the two large doors open to the shop, allowing the fresh morning air to clear the smell.

He pointed to a seat near the table where he worked and they both sat down. He spoke in Latin with a strong accent and the boy paid close attention to catch every word. The old man's raspy voice only made it more difficult to understand him.

"What you wrote," he said, "is something that should be learned by everyone." He stood up again and headed for the door. "Allow me a few moments," he said and walked into the alley and up the stairs to his home.

Clearly this old man did not hear me—he does not even know I don't have the book.

Felix was frustrated. Now this man, too, was suggesting he share his writing with others. He wished he never lost sight of the book in the first place.

A few minutes later, Ephraim returned with two steaming jars and handed one to the boy. The jar was hot and the boy held it with both hands to warm himself as he still shivered from the night spent outside. As he took a sip, the bitter liquid warmed his mouth and chest and continued into his belly. It was the first time the boy had ever tasted tea.

The man took his own seat and made himself comfortable. "I am sorry for sticking my nose where it does not belong, but when you and Haziq came yesterday, I looked through your writings." He took another sip from his tea and set his cup down.

"I lost the book!" Felix exclaimed.

The old man sat silent for a few moments before he spoke. "Written word has no power. Only when applied, does the word become alive," he said.

"You look worried, boy. If your writings were so dear to you, you would not be afraid to lose them. The words you have written give you freedom and they have power only because they are alive in your heart. Write them again." The old man had challenged Felix.

"I, too, have written many words in my life time," he pointed to a pile of scrolls. "Only the ones I made alive in the mind have stuck with me. Your personal declarations are something every man can learn from. The stories and parables you included give them life."

"No one has ever seen them," the boy replied, "Only two men besides yourself even know about my writing. Haziq knows that I have been writing—he suggested I do so in the first place but he has never seen them. And the other is the Jew who healed me. He had not seen my writing but somehow seemed to know."

The old man sat and stared out into the alley. Felix admired the way these men spoke: Haziq, the Jew from the hill, and this transcriber. They thought more than they spoke, unlike men he knew back in Rome who blurted out whatever came to mind. He had always considered Romans to be intelligent people but the more time he spent with the Arab and these Jews, the more he realized he was wrong.

"The thing that happened to you, it is a miracle from God," said Ephraim.

"It is," the boy nodded, "I only have the Jew to thank!"

Ephraim stared at him. "What will you do now?" he asked. Assuming the man was asking about where he was going to go from here, the boy replied, "I will stay with Haziq for as long as he lets me. I have nowhere to go. He has taught me so many things, and I am in great debt to him. I would like to help him fill your order and come back with it to deliver to you…"

The old man interrupted him. "What will you do now that God has given you freedom from your curse?"

The boy stopped. The Jew who had healed him once again came to his mind and he remembered his dream from the ship. He did not want to tell Ephraim about his dream or what the Jew from the hill had asked him to do. It frightened him because he had no clue how he would possibly teach others.

He was afraid and the image of the people from the dream leaving, one by one, as he attempted to speak only stirred the fear. All he wanted to do was learn how to sell from Haziq so that he could buy land for his olive trees.

"You must write again so that others may learn,"

Ephraim said. "Fate brought you here, there is no doubt about it. Every man has his purpose, you may think yours is one thing but what you had in your book needs to be taught.

"You have been equipped through your journey of self-discovery with these principles and you have your powerful story. Now you have been gifted with something most people have possessed since birth and still have not learned how to use with intelligence—the gift of speech."

Felix sat back in his chair and set his cup down as well. He was not going to escape this now. The harder he tried to push the possibility away with every excuse, the stronger the feeling began to swell in his chest.

It was the feeling that only came when he knew he must face his fear and there was no way out. It was the same feeling he would get when he approached people in search of a job back home. He felt it when he entered the office of the army general the day he turned 17. And when he approached this very man, just a few days earlier, with a blank book and the note.

Haziq had told him again and again that it was this feeling that he must not run from but instead, run towards. "When it scares the *kara* out of you," Haziq had said with his accent, "it means you are doing exactly what you need to be doing. Never shy away from what scares you most."

He and Ephraim stared at each other.

"If I were you, I would take a lesson from an old man like me, and I would not deny the call," Ephraim said.

"Many people will spend their entire lives seeking even one word from God, but you... you He has embraced."

"Look around this shop," he said, sweeping his arm in front of him, "This is what I do, this is what I am good at. Let me make copies of your book once you have written it again. I will hire helpers. When you and Haziq deliver my order, bring me double of what I asked and I will use it to make many copies of your writings. You will place a price on your book and you will sell it in the markets.

"Felix, look at what is before you," he said. "Don't keep this wisdom from the world."

Would anyone really care for my writings? Would anyone really learn from them? The book is gone, will I even be able to write it again?

He was so young that older people would not take him seriously. He had never written anything before. But Ephraim saw something in his writings.

He looked at the man, "If people wanted to buy my book, I would need to pay Haziq for the book and you for making the copies. I don't have money."

Now that he saw the boy was interested, Ephraim pushed his tea aside. "I will take a small fraction of each sale you make. The price of a blank book from Haziq— that will be your responsibility."

The boy began to imagine people reading his book.

Could this be what the Jew spoke about when he pointed at the book on the hill?

Maybe Haziq could teach me to sell it. With every book sold, I'd be ordering another from him, which means that Haziq's desire to get his new creation to the world will also be realized.

Perhaps this was the way he could make enough money to buy land for his trees. The thoughts rushed through his mind and he wanted to be back at the inn to tell Haziq about Ephraim's plan.

But he did not know if he would be able to write again, the way he did before. When he'd written each declaration before, the principle had been fresh in his mind.

***

"It is good that you are excited—this is necessary—but your success will depend entirely on you. On your persistence and determination, long after the excitement wears off," came the typical response from Haziq.

Haziq leaned back in his seat on the roof of the inn where they spent their evenings of meals, wine, and the man's occasional pipe smoking. He gazed over the city and then turned to the south, facing the hills and lands that stretched far beyond Jerusalem's walls.

After a few minutes he spoke. "I was afraid for a long time that I would no longer be given the chance to pass on these principles. Then I met you, a scared mute runaway with no direction and no purpose. When I spoke of them I thought I might be wasting my breath but it did me good to get them out of my old head and share them with someone.

"I have many regrets in life," he continued. "And as I said before, one of them is that I never taught them to anyone else. I hoarded them for myself. They were my guidance to gaining wealth, making better habits, and creating a life that is worth living.

"I was wrong. I was wrong about you. I now know why I met you on that dock. I believed it was an omen but I had no idea what would come of it. It may scare you—and it won't be easy to be vulnerable with your deepest thoughts. But if anyone has the ability to share this gold, this mental wealth, with the world, it is you. You must write again."

Chapter 14.

A story is written

When one has a purpose to fill, sleep suddenly becomes less important and appealing.

The boy was up early again. It was becoming easier for him to wake up and he was making a habit of jumping out quickly before the bed could lure him back in.

To his surprise, Haziq was already outside and had the donkey hitched to the cart. He also had a horse with his packs strapped to each side of it. "Where are we going?" the boy asked, puzzled as to why the man had not told him about their plans the night before.

"Just me," Haziq said, feeding the donkey as he spoke and still not looking up at the boy.

"You are going to stay here. You are going to write. Ephraim will teach you and you will continue to write until the book is ready for the world to see. I have paid for your stay here at the inn in advance." He reached into his pack and handed the boy a small leather satchel. The jingle of the coins and the weight of the sack let the boy know it was more than he needed, or certainly, had earned.

"This is for you. Use it for meals, ink, and anything else you may need. Pay Ephraim every time you use his paper and ink—they are costly. Find a better way to tell your stories so that all can relate and all can understand and apply the principles and, even the lowest of people can interpret them," he said.

"Where are you going!?" the boy asked again, still holding onto the satchel of coins uncomfortably. He did not feel right taking from the man, but knew he would need money.

"I am going home. I have orders to fill now and I need to get books prepared for you as well. You will not pay me for any books until they sell and I will only take the price for a blank book. It pleases me to see that already, you have created a need for the books. It will be used exactly as I have hoped," he spoke as he tightened straps and made sure the loads were balanced.

The boy kept silent. He had already learned that words were empty. As a mute, he could express his gratitude more meaningfully, because his face showed it all. After he was able to speak, the words he used rarely expressed the depth of what he truly felt. He did not attempt to thank Haziq for everything; he feared that anything he would say would only take away from how he felt inside. At this moment, his smile showed his appreciation and that was all he could do.

"I do not know how long it will take, but when I am back, we will be ready to proceed," Haziq said, as he climbed onto the horse and tugged on the donkey's lead.

Normally Haziq wore long robes and expensive garments. The man enjoyed flaunting fine clothing and it was probably the reason he was so successful in selling clothing, too, the boy thought. He made the garments look even more prestigious than their own beautiful design already did.

This morning, he was dressed more like an Arabian soldier than a wealthy merchant. He'd strapped a sword to his waist and only his eyes showed through the head-cover that came down to his eyebrows and hid his beard. It would keep him warm on cold mornings and protect him from the sun's heat in the day.

He would not be making many stops between here and Caesarea and that must have been the reason he acquired a horse. It would be a hasty trip.

Felix watched the man ride off into the distance until he could see only the silhouettes of him, the horse and the cart, eventually dissolving around a bend.

He was afraid. He realized the man was in a hurry to bring back the books to Jerusalem because he wanted to bring the boy's writing to the world. Haziq and Ephraim had given him confidence with their encouragement and vision. They allowed him to imagine the possibility of success, were it to come, but he feared that he would fail them. The man was leaving on his account, in a hurry, and traveling alone through a dangerous region and in a dangerous time.

What if they were wrong?
What if no one buys the book?

He felt sick to his stomach and took a deep breath to calm his thoughts. Though fear like this had crippled him for so long, he wouldn't give in to it.

"Words spoken set life in motion," he repeated the first declaration out loud. He would need to reaffirm his own faith in himself if he was to handle such a task.

Ephraim and Haziq were much older and wiser than he was; Surely they could deal with failure if it were to come and, besides, there was not much he could do now. It was too late to say no. It was too late to change his mind.

***

When he arrived at the shop, Ephraim was already working by candlelight. When he saw the boy at the entrance, he smiled and invited him in. They spent the entire day working in the shop and the only time the boy stepped out was to stretch his legs and his writing hand.

Ephraim instructed Felix to write his entire story. As far back as he could remember, right up to now. Every significant incident, everything that made him cry, and everything that brought him joy, he wrote and rewrote.

He closed his eyes and recited the declarations from memory, and then wrote them down.

Every hour or so the old man would come and look over his shoulder. He would point to something and the boy would have to restart.

"Do not try to be poetic," he said, "tell your story. The

moment that you try to tell it in a way that you think people might like, is the moment you must stop and start over. Everyone's story is unique yet most people bury theirs because they are ashamed of it, they do not realize the power in it. They fear being different, and with that, they surrender their experience."

The boy spent more time staring at the paper than he did writing. He argued with every voice in his head that told him not to be vulnerable. It was frightening enough when Ephraim had read it and it would be much more frightening to let the world see it.

He wrote about all of the nights he cried in frustration and anger. All of the days he spent alone, in fear of yet another rejection. And his decision to run away from everything he knew because he had quit on his dream.

He did not understand why the old man wanted him to include every detail, he could not see the purpose in it.

"I can certainly see why someone would want to learn about the principles as they have changed my life and could help others, but why would anyone be interested in my misery? It is only a pathetic recollection of my lack of persistence!" he said.

Ephraim replied, "Many people become slaves to destructive thought, but it is your perspective and your journey to victory, out of defeat, that can change their lives.

"When you show your weaknesses, some may laugh and even call you weak but deep down, they will know what you speak of. Being vulnerable connects mankind. This is how we understand each other.

"People want to find themselves in your story, this is how they decide to follow you. When you reveal that you are on the same journey, only then, will they trust you enough to listen. Emotions are not a sign of weakness; they are a sign of humanness. Never forget that. If you want success, in any aspect of life, learn to connect."

The man scarcely looked up from his work but he never stopped speaking. The boy knew about keeping his own mouth shut.

I must have seemed much wiser when I was unable to speak.

Every morning the boy would head to Ephraim's shop. By the end of each day, his hands were covered in ink. Over and over, Ephraim pressed him. "Don't try to be clever. Just as you wrote to yourself in simplicity, do it again."

In the evenings, he headed for the hill. He had been hoping to meet the Jew again and every once in a while, turned to check behind him. The boy had more questions about God. He spent the last daylight hours gazing over the city and the countryside that surrounded it.

He was changing. Ephraim was pushing him to expect perfection.

In Rome, when he was faced with struggle, he'd always quit and move on to a new thing. Now his desire to prove the men right pushed him to great lengths. Often he had wanted to quit, but refused to because they had faith in him. Giving up was not an option. He would not fail them and anytime the thought of failure crept into his mind, it only made him angry. He noticed that it only drove him harder and his persistence increased.

Some evenings, when Ephraim called an end to the day the boy stayed in the shop and continued to write into the night.

If he had remained alone, he would surely have been a beggar by now, or worse, dead. But his new friends, much older than him, had painted a picture of a life worth living.

The quality of company you keep, directly influences the quality of life you will live, he thought to himself.

The days passed and the Passover festival began in Jerusalem. The Jewish holiday called for various purification periods and other traditions that Ephraim followed, often leaving the boy alone in the shop. He'd approved the pages the boy had written, one by one. The book was nearly finished.

Getting his story out of his head and onto paper had given the boy a look at his life from a brand-new perspective. He remembered moments that he had long ago forgotten. He remembered words people said, looks they gave, and the negativity that had occupied his mind, continually reaffirming his inability to create the life he desired. With each painful recollection, he realized how much time he had spent, soaking in his own misery.

He remembered the fateful day when he was 6 years old. The woman who had raised him at the orphanage had attempted to explain to him why he did not have a mother and father like the children in the city. It was the loneliest day of his life.

He cried at the memories of trying to speak like the other kids. He covered his face in shame when he recalled Licinia, who had attempted to lift him up and encourage him, only to get an angry look from him out of frustration and self-pity.

His disability was once his most prized excuse and now as he looked back, he regretted the moments he spent justifying himself with it. He regretted the time he spent looking at what others had and he himself was missing. If he would have learned to work around his limitation, he could have done things differently as he grew, instead of building it into his identity.

He would not trade this journey to his new life for anything in the world. He knew he was exactly where he needed to be but was haunted by thoughts of the girl and the missed opportunities, and the joy and the beauty of each day that he had squandered. Regret is a painful thing, he thought. And now, it was his greatest fear, to live even a single day in this world and look back on it with regret.

This perspective allowed him to press on every day in the shop, working towards his greatest achievement yet. If he kept true to his declarations and lived them out daily, the dream of owning his own olive orchards would surely come to pass. For now, it was the time to work. If the men believed in him, he would believe in himself.

"I will turn my pain into the greatest story ever told," he proclaimed.

Chapter 15.

The place of the skull

"I can't believe they're still celebrating," murmured the boy as he shut the door of the shop.

But the commotion only got louder and he heard chanting in Hebrew. The boy didn't understand the language but the shouting did not sound joyful—more like jeering—and he stepped out into the street to see an enormous crowd mobbing a group of soldiers.

People ran from every direction to join the mob in the already crowded street. Others looked down from their roofs and squeezed out of windows to watch the procession. The boy saw Roman soldiers shoving people aside and the sound of a cracking whip temporarily cleared the way.

He quickly ran up the steps that led to Ephraim's door and pulled himself up the wall and onto the roof. Running up to the edge, he looked over and immediately recognized what he was witnessing. They were leading a criminal through the streets after he had been sentenced for execution.

But why was there so much interest from the crowd? Surely this was not an uncommon event.

A familiar feeling came over him. It had only been a few months since he was on post for the last execution before leaving Rome. Those experiences brought back a sinking feeling to his stomach. It had always scared him no matter how many times he witnessed it.

One thing was odd: this criminal was badly beaten and carried his own cross. His robe was covered in blood from his shoulders to his feet, and his face, too, was bleeding. The boy could see that one of the man's eyes was nearly swollen shut.

He must have done something terrible.

Often, the Romans would sentence a man to a flogging, sometimes to the point of death, but never did they flog a man before hanging him on a cross.

The man stumbled several times under the weight of the heavy beam that lay across his back. Every time he fell the soldiers cracked the whip over his body and he would slowly raise himself up to his feet. The boy wondered why the large crowd was so passionate, cheering on the brutality of the soldiers. Perhaps the criminal had murdered someone during the festival. How else could he invoke such hatred from the angry mob?

A moment later Ephraim joined him on the roof. He had come up to investigate the commotion, too.

"It is a crucifixion," the boy said, pointing to the

crowd that was now directly below them in the street.

"I see that," Ephraim replied, "This must be the man who blasphemed God."

The boy stared at the man with his jaw open. "They are executing him for blaspheming!?" he asked, confused about why Roman soldiers would care about a Jewish man blaspheming a Jewish God.

With the Roman occupation of the region, they left each religion to believe in the gods they chose... so why were they involved now?

"I have heard of this man—he claims to be a son of God," Ephraim spoke again answering the boy's question before he had a chance to ask.

"The religious people hate him because he has caused them a lot of trouble, especially during this year's festival. He also cost them a lot of money. Religion is how they control the people, it's how they make their money," he said.

"He has been teaching a new way to God—a way that does not require rules, money, or sacrifices from them and the religious men don't like that. These people are sheep. They follow those who have imprisoned them with fear and they reject anything that is different from the way they have always known it to be. They don't think for themselves." The man's nostrils flared and a frown came over his face. He was disgusted by what he was witnessing.

"I myself have never seen the man," said Ephraim, "but they say he has given people a new hope so the temple officials fear him—he loosens their grip on the people."

He continued to look on as the crowd pushed farther through the street toward the gate.

"What are they chanting?" Felix asked. *"Crucify him,"* the old man replied.

Pointing at the crowd, he looked at the boy again. "This… This is why you must not fear people seeing your writing. People like this need your book."

"Look at them, they only know one way and they didn't even choose on their own. It was taught to them. They must be taught to think for themselves. They are killing a man for offending God, yet they do not know God. They do not understand that the way of God is the way of love, not this zealous and misguided passion. Look at what religion has done," he continued. "It imprisons their minds and they in turn, imprison those around them. It has turned lions to sheep and they follow the wrong shepherds."

"They will kill me, too!" the boy shouted, looking down at the crowd. Ephraim responded, "No. You have written in simplicity. You have written the principles in a way that any simple-minded man can understand and apply. You do not wage war against religion or any God, you present the principles in a way that when applied, one can truly find a better way to live. Now, me they would kill, that is why I keep my old mouth shut.

"You can't fill old wineskins with new wine, they would burst. But there is another generation rising up after this one, and if not taught a different way, they will continue the vicious cycle."

They stood and watched in silence as the mob raged, and suddenly the boy's heart sank. The long, now bloodied robe the criminal was wearing and the rope tied around the waist were familiar. He sprinted and grabbing onto the edge of the roof, leaped to the top of the stairs over the door and ran down the steps, barely staying upright as he skipped steps.

He ran towards the back end of the mob and pushed into the crowd.

He looks like the Jew who healed me! It can't be him!

The thought repeated itself over and over. Was this the man that had mercy on him on the mountain and showed a love towards him that he had never known?

He shoved passed people and ducked under elbows, making his way closer to the center.

"Sir!!" he screamed towards the man under the beam. "Sir!!" A soldier grabbed him around the chest and threw him back into the crowd. He stood up again and continued to follow as close as he could get, trying to see the man's badly beaten face.

He ran ahead of the crowd, hoping to get a closer look as the procession drew closer. They were near the gate, and the inn where he and Haziq were living was only a few hundred yards away. One of the soldiers had his back to the crowd and the boy, gathering enough courage, squeezed between people again and ran up to the man, grabbing his robe.

"Sir, are you the one from the mount!?" he yelled, trying to get the man to hear him over the chanting of the crowd. "Do you remember me!?"

One eye was nearly swollen shut but through the blood, the brown eyes of the man locked with the boy's. It was him.

"I... remember you," the man struggled to speak under the weight of the wood. The boy dropped to his knees and slid his shoulder under the cross beam to take some of the weight on himself.

As soon as he grabbed the cross, he felt a loud thud against his ear and seeing nothing but darkness, crumpled to the ground.

A soldier stood over him and began to beat him with a long club and the boy held his hands over his face for cover.

"The next time you come up, you will join him!" the man screamed and after kicking the boy one last time, joined the rest of the soldiers.

The gash on his throbbing head was bleeding, but he gathered himself off of the dirt road and ran towards the inn. Haziq would be back by now and could do something about this, he thought, and ran as hard as he could. His body ached but he did not stop.

He burst into Haziq's room and the man dropped his book as soon as he saw the bleeding boy. Out of breath and hardly able to speak, he managed to scream a few words, "The man... the man that healed me... they are going to kill him!"

Haziq ran outside to see the procession head south onto the road that curved upward toward a cliff. Felix followed him and they caught up with the crowd a few hundred yards away as it made its way up the steep hill. Haziq's face remained grim and, despite the boy's hysteria, he had not said a word as they hurried.

The crowd stopped at the top, but kept chanting. There, the soldiers had stretched the Jew's arms as he lay on the beam. The sound of the steel hammers against the nails echoed through the valley as the nails drove deep into the wood. There was already a large group of soldiers on the hill and two other criminals hung from their crosses. The boy and Haziq walked past a tattered sign that read "*Golgotha*," in Hebrew and "*Skull Hill*," in Latin.

The boy fell to the ground and began to vomit.

Haziq grabbed him with both hands and roughly yanked him to his feet, shaking him as he yelled: "When we get up there you shut your mouth or they will execute you as well!"

As Felix slowly followed Haziq, he realized there was nothing the wise man could do for the Jew on the cross.

He could see the mountain of olive trees from here and he stared at it, trying not to look at the naked man nailed to the beam. Tears streamed down his face and did not stop flowing.

An anger welled up in him so fierce—the Romans, the Arabs, these Jews… he hated all of these people at that moment.

The crowd remained until a heavy rain began. It beat down on them without ceasing and they dispersed. In his dream, it was Felix who attempted to speak, and the Jew was the only one left after everyone had walked away.

Now, it was the man on the cross who watched the crowd leave one by one and only the boy, Haziq, a weeping woman, and a handful of soldiers were left standing, drenched in the rain.

Several times the Jew, gathered his strength, pulled himself up on the cross and cried out in Hebrew, *"Eloi Eloi lama sabachthani."* Each time the boy ran up, hoping it was him the man wanted to speak to.

After a few hours the dying man tilted his head towards the boy and Haziq, whose head was down and his eyes closed.

"Let go of the hate that grips your heart boy, it is poison," he choked out the words. "They do not know any better. Do what I have asked of you."

The boy stared up blankly, there were no more tears in his eyes, there was nothing left to cry. But as the man spoke, he nodded, not knowing how he could do what the man was asking of him. The soldiers quit talking amongst themselves and looked with surprise as the man spoke in their native language to the boy.

Felix stood and clung to every word, remembering how when the men being executed back in Rome tried to speak with him, he would run away.

Felix did not want to sell his book anymore. He wanted to tear it to pieces the minute he saw it again. None of these cowardly, cruel people deserved to learn the principles that had changed his own life. People with such arrogance and blindness would never value his precious declarations anyway.

But the man on the cross had insisted. He felt torn. Then a sudden realization came over him.

I, too, was once like them. I was once filled with rage and my failures only turned me into a bitter man, accusing everyone around me of being luckier than myself.

I, too, not so long ago had no idea what the purpose of my existence was. I, too, did not know what was required of a man to discover an extraordinary life, to find his true purpose. I, too, went through life, aimlessly following the crowd.

There were two types of people, he thought. There was this passionate and misdirected mob who clung to a belief just to be a part of something bigger than themselves, just to believe in something.

And then there were people like him, or like he used to be. People who had nothing to cling to at all, who wandered through life aimlessly with no particular direction or guidance, and no destination. All they had was a hope that one day life would drop their dreams into their lap.

Both types missed the mark. Both could learn much from these golden principles.

That must have been why the man, now dying above him, was so persistent in his mission for the boy.

He sat down in the mud, his face in his knees. The cold rain ran down his neck as he shivered but refused to move. Haziq also remained. He was mostly silent and only muttered a few words to himself.

Finally Haziq approached the foot of the cross and looked up at the man. With a shaky voice and trembling hands, he spoke: "I am a praying man... I do not follow the religion of the Jews, I do not follow the religion I was raised with, I just pray. I pray to God and He guides me..."

He looked down and stood silently for a moment before speaking again, "Are you... are you the one He has spoken of? Are you the one we have been waiting for?"

The man's chest slowly expanded and he gathered the strength to speak again: "It is not by your wisdom that this had been revealed to you, but by your faith."

Haziq knelt on the ground and began to weep bitterly.

A chill ran down Felix's spine. This man he had known for such a short time but so intensely, had always been so strong. He never let the surprises of life sway him too far either way—unflinching when the ship was attacked by pirates, not rejoicing when he had great success in his sales. Now he was on the ground, sobbing.

The Jew looked down at the two of them as they sat in the mud, created by blood and water. Once again their eyes locked and the boy sat, trembling in the cold. The entire universe seemed to burst through the man's eyes and into the boy's soul. It was now that he understood something that Haziq had already known. He was looking into the eyes of God.

Chapter 16.

"You must choose to believe"

The Jew drew one more breath and shouted in Hebrew, eyes lifted to the sky. Felix waited for Haziq to translate the words, but he remained on the ground, his head in his hands. The man on the cross exhaled deeply and his chin fell against his chest. He was dead.

***

"Faith is one principle which cannot be taught, but it is the most precious of them all. This is one that each man must discover on his own." The setting sun turned Haziq's skin gold as he spoke.

The boy nodded. After looking into the eyes of the man on the cross, he knew there was one thing he had been missing: He did not have faith in the very source that had given him life.

A week had passed since the crucifixion of the Jew

and the two sat on the sundeck of the inn's roof. The boy's book was nearly complete and his mind was restless; he wanted to add something but couldn't find the words.

"To not believe in God is to not believe in the power that man contains. It is to hold one's breath and ignore the very source that refills the lungs. It is to be a fish in the water, asking 'where is the water?' when in fact, it lives and moves and has its being in it.

"One must not follow religion, rules, or other men who teach only a fraction of the truth," Haziq added. "One must seek a connection to this source that is unique to him alone and only then, when he is not hindered by the perceptions and ideas of others, will he fully understand it."

Haziq turned to the boy. "There is a parable I have heard long ago," he said. "A blind man touches the elephant's tale and says, 'The elephant is a long and round creature, like a snake.' Another touches the elephant's ear and says, 'The elephant is a thin and flat creature, like a stingray.' Yet another touches its trunk and proclaims, 'The elephant is like a pillar!'

"The experiences of the three men have limited their understanding of the elephant," Haziq explained. "None of them have grasped the entirety of the animal. It is because of this blindness that separation of humanity continues, that wars rage, and a man turns on another. They have failed to see God.

"Don't silence that still small voice with which He speaks. It is not in the thunder and lightning that He speaks, it is in the whisper of the wind. It is in the warmth of the sun on the face of the broken hearted. It is in the budding of a young olive tree. Open your heart and believe."

Felix had one more declaration to write.

"

Declaration #11: You must choose to believe.

Though I do not see, I will choose to believe.

Though I do not hear, I will choose to believe.

Though I do not understand, I will choose to believe.

It is not in the wisdom of man that the creator resides, it is in the simplicity of a child that He lives.

It is not by logic that I will understand, it is by the broken spirit that I will learn to believe.

The world is thrown into turmoil by those who believe and those who disagree and still I will not learn from either. I will seek His presence in all that I do and it is there that I will learn to believe.

It is with His breath that my lungs are filled.

It is by His hand that my heart pumps as I sleep.

It is by His will that my mind can achieve whatever it conceives.

I will choose to believe.

***

News about the book spread quickly through the entire region. And the three did not rest. Ephraim and Haziq relentlessly visited every merchant in the city through the following months as the boy and others worked day and night at the shop, making copies.

"Felix the Roman: The mute who speaks" was written on the cover of each book.

People wanted to read about the boy who was healed by the crucified man from Galilea.

They lined up at the shop to purchase books, but the boy soon realized that it was him they came to see. Rumor had spread that the executed man had risen from the dead and now the boy's story was even more sought after. Everyone wanted to see the workings of a miracle and would ask him if he really was mute his entire life. If the boy had indeed been healed, wouldn't that make the rumors about the man true? They wanted to know.

The Roman leaders overseeing the occupation in Jerusalem invited the three men for a meal. They had learned of Felix, a Roman native. The boy was of great value to them because of his growing popularity. The relationship between the Jews and the Romans became even more strained after the execution of the man.

The Jews were rebelling against the religious leaders who lost their hold of the people, a centurion explained. The Roman army desperately needed something to bridge the gap between the Jews and those attempting to keep the chaos under control.

The boy was their answer.

He was a Roman respected by Jews. His book continued to spread through the region, written in both Hebrew and Latin. Thousands of copies were already on order and soon, strategic merchants began to place orders to sell in cities where word had not yet spread.

One day as the boy was sitting in his usual place on the mountain, giving himself time away from the chaos that was his new life, a middle-aged woman approached him. He recognized her as a servant of the old man who owned the land and the olive trees.

Felix apologized and stood up to leave.

"The land and house are being sold," she said. "The owner is about to die. He has no family to inherit this land. It is alright for you to be here."

Overwhelmed with joy, he hurried back to the inn, where they were still staying.

His pouch was now filled with gold. He had not been spending any of his ever-increasing earnings because there was nothing he wanted more than the olive orchard he'd envisioned for so long. He had been searching for land to purchase but no place satisfied his soul like his spot on this mount.

He brought his pouch to the old man, who was happy to sell to someone who loved the land as he once did. Before he left, Felix asked the servants to stay and he would pay their same wages, plus more.

The boy stepped right into his new life. With the servants he took care of the house and farmed the fields. They sold the majority of the harvest and the boy used whatever was left over for himself.

They bottled rich olive oil and packaged baskets full of raw fruit. They sold the olives every way imaginable and the boy learned the entire process from the workers.

He spent his days in the fields, learning to use the olive press as he worked alongside them. He insisted on doing the most dirty and difficult parts of the job. The simplicity of the soil sifting through his hands and sticking under his finger nails took his mind away from all there was to do in his new world.

He spoke to the soil and told it of the trees it would raise to life.

He often shared his story with the workers and explained his early dreams about planting olive trees.

"Just when it seems like the olive tree will never produce, it brings forth more fruit than can be contained," he would say. This was his favorite memory of the girl.

He spent many evenings alone on the hill after the workers went home for the day, hoping that maybe one day the man who healed him would be back. He hoped the rumors of his resurrection were true.

Every month the Romans organized festivities to lessen the friction in the city and the boy agreed to speak at the events. Crowds gathered to hear him speak—Jews, Arabs, and Romans alike.

Every time he was about to begin, he remembered his dream and fought to calm his heart from the paralyzing fear that never went away. Then, he shared his story and he taught the principles that Haziq had given to him, sharing the parables that Haziq and the Jew named Jesus had taught him.

***

Late one afternoon, he was sitting in the shade of the house's lattice work when a servant approached him.

"Adoni Felix, someone stands at the door requesting to speak with you."

Assuming it was someone wanting to see him because of the book, he told the servant to give them a copy and send them off. But they refused to leave. In frustration the boy marched to the door, when he reached it, the breath was cut from his chest.

He would know the long dark curls and green eyes of the precious girl from the orphanage anywhere.

"It *is* you!" she exclaimed, and she ran into the house, embracing him as the nervous servant stood nearby.

That evening, they sat outside by a crackling fire, drinking wine Felix had imported from his new friend in Phoenix.

The rows of olive trees stretched before them and just below, the torches in the city flickered in the evening dusk. The scorching heat of the day had gradually cooled into a warm evening breeze and it gently blew the flame of the fire to and fro.

He listened to her speak and every few minutes, turned his head to look away to the hills, hiding the tears in his eyes. It took great effort to keep himself from breaking into a sob. He thought he would never see the girl again, but here she was and his heart was ready to burst.

Licinia told him that the book had made its way to

Rome. She was working at the orphanage now, helping the other women take care of the children. One day, one of the women approached her and showed her the book. "It can't be our Felix… can it?" she had said.

After he left, they had no idea of his whereabouts. When she read the book she knew it was him, the hopeless mute from the orphanage. She spent all of her earnings to pay for her trip. When she made it to Jerusalem, she had asked for him and they told her he was the man who owned the mountain of olives.

They talked long into the night and the boy told her everything that had happened since he left Rome. When he told her about the day he first spoke, she cried.

He told her of his transformation and the principles he had learned and taught. He told her all about the man who healed him. The man who, through his death, had turned the entire kingdom upside down. No Roman, no Jew, no religion had control of the people now. There was a freedom spreading like wild-fire. A freedom of the heart and mind, one that could never be stripped away.

He glanced down at his calloused hands, stained with ink that hadn't washed out. He had come a long way from being the frightened and hopeless mute. But the real battle was one that had been won in his mind. Since then, he had become a sailor, a salesman, an author, and now a farmer of the most precious trees in the world.

It is true, he thought, *to find the extraordinary life, one must understand that words spoken set life in motion.*

One must always live with the end in mind.

He must, in all things, be filled with gratitude.

Each day, he must give of himself more than he ever has before.

He must not blame anyone but himself.

He must develop a burning desire for the thing he wants to achieve.

He must take action towards that thing.

He is to always persist if he wishes for that thing to be realized.

He needs to understand that he is a creature of habit.

Choosing to live in love will set him free.

He must only choose to believe.

He had lived into his name. He was *"Lucky."* He was *"Successful."*

If one desires the extraordinary life, one must ask, and it will be given to him. One must seek, and he will find it. One must knock, and it will be opened to him.

Felix and Licinia remained on the patio late into the night. They laughed and drank and poured more wine until the vessel was empty. Then he took his sandals off and ran through the olive orchard and she followed him, just like that day when they were 11 years old.

The Mount of Olives

About the author

Michael was born in Soviet Russia and came to the United States at two years old with his parents and siblings as a political refugee. He grew up in the small town of Washougal, near Portland Oregon, and still calls the area his home.

He continues to pursue his dream of writing and speaking in hopes of helping people discover a better way to live.

Acknowledgments

Editor:

All credit goes to my editor, Madeleine Eno. She has taken this story to another level to say the least, and has truly turned something ordinary into something extraordinary!

Meet Madeleine here: **www.InTheWritePlace.com**

Designer:

My sister-in-law, Sulamita Ivanov, deserves all credit for the simple, yet beautiful cover design as well as the life-giving sketches inside.

Meet Sulamita here: Instagram **@sulamitaiva** and here: **www.Sulamita.co**

Made in United States
North Haven, CT
23 November 2021

11196860R00098